M000248360

Latin

ONE

FOR COMMON ENTRANCE

N. R. R. Oulton

GALORE PARK

AN HACHETTE UK COMPANY

About the author

Nicholas Oulton read History at Oriel College, Oxford and has an MA in Classics from London University. He taught Latin and Greek for ten years before writing the *So you really want to learn Latin* course and founding Galore Park in 1998.

Acknowledgements

The author and the publisher would like to thank Stephen Anderson for his generosity and support in producing this book.

Stephen Anderson studied classics at Trinity College, Dublin and St John's College, Cambridge. From 1980 to 2015 he taught at Winchester College, where he was Head of Classics from 1984 to 2008 and subsequently Senior Tutor. In October 2015 he took up a new post as Lecturer in Classical Languages at New College, Oxford.

The publishers would like to thank the following for permission to reproduce copyright material:

Photo credits p1 ©bajabandito - Fotolia **p7** © The Art Archive / Alamy Stock Photo **p21** © javarman - Fotolia.com **p36** © The Art Archive / Alamy Stock Photo **p50** © Lanmas / Alamy Stock Photo **p62** © Lanmas / Alamy Stock Photo **p72** © Ivy Close Images / Alamy Stock Photo **p79** ©Getty Images/iStockphoto/Thinkstock **p81** © The Art Archive / Alamy Stock Photo **p106** © Lanmas / Alamy Stock Photo

Every effort has been made to trace all copyright holders, but if any have been inadvertently overlooked, the publishers will be pleased to make the necessary arrangements at the first opportunity.

Although every effort has been made to ensure that website addresses are correct at time of going to press, Galore Park cannot be held responsible for the content of any website mentioned in this book. It is sometimes possible to find a relocated web page by typing in the address of the home page for a website in the URL window of your browser.

Hachette UK's policy is to use papers that are natural, renewable and recyclable products and made from wood grown in sustainable forests. The logging and manufacturing processes are expected to conform to the environmental regulations of the country of origin.

Orders: please contact Bookpoint Ltd, 130 Park Drive, Milton Park, Abingdon, Oxon OX14 4SE. Telephone: (44) 01235 827720. Fax: (44) 01235 400454. Email education@bookpoint.co.uk Lines are open from 9 a.m. to 5 p.m., Monday to Saturday, with a 24-hour message answering service. Visit our website at www.galorepark.co.uk for details of other revision guides for Common Entrance, examination papers and Galore Park publications.

ISBN: 9781471867378

Text copyright © N.R.R. Oulton 2016

First published in 2016 by

Galore Park Publishing Ltd,

An Hachette UK Company

Carmelite House

50 Victoria Embankment

London EC4Y 0DZ

Impression number   10 9 8 7 6 5 4 3 2 1

Year   2020 2019 2018 2017 2016

Cover photo © powerofforever - istockphoto.com

Typeset in India

Printed in Italy

A catalogue record for this title is available from the British Library.

Contents

Introduction

Latin is a language, as dead as dead can be.
It killed the ancient Romans, and now it's killing me.

Well, if this is true, why are we learning Latin now?

At the height of their power, around two thousand years ago, the Romans ruled an empire which extended to most of modern Europe and beyond to Palestine, Egypt and north Africa. Their skill at engineering and construction was unmatched until the 20th century, and their form of administration, considering the size of their empire, was remarkable. But they could also be a cruel, bloodthirsty lot, who enjoyed watching animals being torn to bits in the arena, or gladiators fighting to the death with tridents.

In this book we will begin to learn the language of the Romans, Latin, which is the basis for so much of our own English language and that of many other European languages. We will learn a little about the origins of Rome, and read stories of her early heroes such as Romulus, Horatius, Cloelia and Mucius Scaevola. We will also learn a little about the Trojan War, which the Romans loved to read about, and Ulysses (whom the Greeks called Odysseus), whose adventures on the way home from Troy inspired some of the greatest literature of the classical age.

To help with the correct pronunciation of Latin, we have marked the vowels on the Latin words where these should be pronounced as long with a mark called a macron (e.g. nārrat, fēmina, īnsula, rogō, tūtus). Occasionally, where people tend to pronounce a vowel as long when it should be short, we have marked it with a mark called a breve, as in the word egŏ which has a short o at the end, not a long one.

When you see Latin in exam papers and practice exercises, and indeed in many other places, these long and short vowels are not marked. However, while you are learning the language, which should be read aloud as often as possible, we hope you will find these marks useful.

Vocabularies for learning are given at the end of each chapter, and a complete set of English–Latin and Latin–English vocabularies is given at the end. There is a summary of all the grammar that you cover in this book at the back, and you will also find there a more detailed guide to pronunciation.

Latin is the most wonderful language, and we hope you enjoy this introductory course.

⃝ Notes on features in this book

Exercise

Exercises are provided to give you plenty of opportunities to practise what you have learned.

> Useful rules and reminders are scattered throughout the book.

The box on the right makes it clear that you are studying a non-linguistic topic required by the ISEB Classics syllabus. Non-linguistic topics are about:

> This topic is part of the Non-Linguistic Studies section of the ISEB syllabus.

- aspects of domestic life in Rome
- early Roman legends
- Roman entertainment
- the Roman army
- Roman Britain
- Greek mythology.

Go further

This heading highlights material that is beyond the requirements of the ISEB syllabus. You do not need to remember this material for your exam, but it will help you understand some interesting aspects of the language.

1 Verbs like amō; personal pronouns

○ Cogitō ergo sum

■ Auguste Rodin's 'The Thinker'

The Latin phrase 'cogitō ergo sum' means 'I think, therefore I am'. In this book we are going to learn to *think*, if not *be*, like the Romans, and we will begin by learning about verbs and the way the Romans used them.

There are two main types of verb: regular and irregular. The first regular verb we are going to learn is amō, which means I love or I like.

◯ Amō – present tense

amō = I love, I like		
1st person singular	am-ō	I love
2nd person singular	amā-s	You (sing.) love
3rd person singular	ama-t	He, she or it loves
1st person plural	amā-mus	We love
2nd person plural	amā-tis	You (pl.) love
3rd person plural	ama-nt	They love

Notice how the **STEM** (the front end) of the verb tells us *what* is being done, and the **ENDINGS** (the back end) tell us *who or what* is doing it.

Verbs can be used in a number of different **TENSES**. The **present tense** tells us what is happening now.

The **present stem** of amō is amā-, which contracts to am- in the first person singular of the present tense.

◯ Verbs like amō

Verbs are divided into four main groups called **CONJUGATIONS**. Verbs of the 1st conjugation go like amō. Thus cantō = I sing and aedificō = I build go:

1st person singular	cant-ō	I sing
2nd person singular	cantā-s	You sing
3rd person singular	canta-t	He, she, it sings
1st person plural	cantā-mus	We sing
2nd person plural	cantā-tis	You sing
3rd person plural	canta-nt	They sing
1st person singular	aedific-ō	I build
2nd person singular	aedificā-s	You build
3rd person singular	aedifica-t	He, she, it builds
1st person plural	aedificā-mus	We build
2nd person plural	aedificā-tis	You build
3rd person plural	aedifica-nt	They build

Notice how cantō and aedificō, written out in the present tense, use exactly the same endings as amō. *All* 1st conjugation verbs copy amō in this way. N.B. The hyphen between the stem and the endings is only given to help you recognise the two parts of the word. You do not need to use hyphens in the exercises that follow.

Exercise 1.1

Write out the present tense of the following verbs, *together with their meanings:*

1 vocō = I call
2 nāvigō = I sail
3 festīnō = I hurry
4 labōrō = I work

Exercise 1.2

Translate into English:

1 cantat.
2 amās.
3 nāvigās.
4 vocātis.
5 aedificant.
6 festīnātis.
7 labōrās.
8 aedificō.
9 cantās.
10 vocat.

Exercise 1.3

Translate into Latin:

1 We love.
2 You (sing.) are sailing.
3 They are hurrying.
4 He sails.
5 She is calling.
6 You (pl.) like.
7 We sing.
8 It sails.
9 You (pl.) build.
10 He is singing.

Exercise 1.4

Translate into English:

1 cantant.
2 amātis.
3 nāvigātis.
4 vocāmus.
5 aedificat.
6 festīnās.
7 labōrātis.
8 vocō.
9 cantāmus.
10 vocant.

Exercise 1.5

Translate into Latin:

1 We are building.

2 They sing.

3 She is hurrying.

4 They sail.

5 We are working.

6 I love.

7 You (pl.) call.

8 He is sailing.

9 We call.

10 You (sing.) are hurrying.

◯ And, but, not

Verbs may be joined by the conjunctions et = 'and' or sed = 'but'. Thus:

amat et cantat = He loves and sings.

They may be made negative by using the adverb nōn = 'not'. Thus:
nōn amat = He does not love.

◯ Personal pronouns

We know who is doing a Latin verb by looking at the verb ending.

E.g. amā**mus** = *we* love.

canta**t** = *he/she* sings.

But sometimes, for emphasis, personal pronouns are used.

Singular		Plural
1st person	egŏ = I	nōs = we
2nd person	tū = you	vōs = you

E.g. egŏ cantō sed tū labōrō.

    I am singing but *you* are working.

1 Verbs like amō; personal pronouns

Exercise 1.6

Translate the following. Some new verbs are used (from Vocabulary 1 at the end of the chapter).

1 rogant et vocant.

2 nōn cantat.

3 vōs spectātis sed nōs cantāmus.

4 festīnātis et labōrātis.

5 vōs nōn vocātis.

6 pugnant et superant.

7 pugnat sed nōs labōrāmus.

8 vocat et festīnat.

9 tū pugnās sed egŏ superō.

10 nōn pugnāmus.

Exercise 1.7

Translate into English:

1 egŏ labōrō sed tū cantās.

2 tū ambulās sed nōs festīnāmus.

3 nōs nāvigāmus et vōs ambulātis.

4 vōs clāmātis.

5 egŏ festīnō sed tū ambulās.

6 vōs nōn cantātis.

7 tū nōn clāmās.

8 nōs labōrāmus et clāmāmus.

9 tū vocās et egŏ cantō.

10 nōs ambulāmus sed vōs festīnātis.

Exercise 1.8

Translate into Latin, using pronouns for emphasis:

1 I work and you (pl.) sing.

2 You (sing.) do not work.

3 We are fighting.

4 I am not walking.

5 We do not sing.

6 You (pl.) are fighting and we are watching.

7 We are building.

8 You (sing.) are hurrying.

9 We sail and you (pl.) fight.

10 I am not shouting.

◯ English derivations

Many English words are derived from Latin ones. It is often possible to work out the meaning of an English word if you recognise the Latin *root* from which it is derived.

E.g. the English adjective *pugnacious* comes from the Latin verb pugnō = I fight and describes someone who likes fighting.

Exercise 1.9

Copy and complete the table below to show the origin of English words. The first one has been done for you.

Latin word	Meaning of Latin word	English word derived from it
amō	I love	amorous
1 spectō		
2 clāmō		
3 labōrō		
4 nāvigō		
5 vocō		

◯ Learning vocabulary

There are 200 words to learn on the Level 1 Common Entrance syllabus, and we are going to learn them at the rate of 20 per chapter. When you learn vocabulary, always make sure that you know the word 'both ways'. In other words, first learn that aedificō means 'I build', but then learn that the Latin for 'I build' is aedificō. You only know the word properly when you can do it both ways.

◯ Vocabulary 1

Latin	English
aedificō	I build
amō	I love, like
cantō	I sing
clāmō	I shout
festīnō	I hurry
labōrō	I work
nāvigō	I sail

Latin	English
parō	I prepare
pugnō	I fight
spectō	I watch
superō	I overcome
vocō	I call
nōn	not
et	and
sed	but
egǒ	I
tū	You (sing.)
nōs	We
vōs	You (pl.)

The origins of Rome

According to legend Rome was founded by Romulus in 753 BC.
However the story starts long before that, dating back to the time of
the Trojan War. The ancient city of Troy was captured and destroyed in
around 1250 BC by a Greek army led by Agamemnon, king of Mycenae.
All its inhabitants were either killed or led into slavery; all, that is,
except for a brave band of men led by the Trojan prince, Aeneas.
This man, the son of the goddess Venus, was ordered to set out from
the burning city, carrying the household gods, with his aged father
Anchises on his back and holding his young son Ascanius (or Iulus)
by the hand. After many adventures and a
long, dangerous journey, during which he met
and fell in love with the Carthaginian Queen,
Dido, Aeneas eventually arrived in Italy.
There he fought with a local prince, Turnus,
for the right to marry Lavinia, daughter of
King Latinus. After defeating Turnus, Aeneas
married the girl and built a new city which he
named Lavinium. The story of Aeneas is told
in Virgil's great epic poem the *Aeneid*.

Aeneas's son, Ascanius, soon left Lavinium
and went off to found his own city. It was
in this city, Alba Longa, many generations
later, that the true founder of Rome, Romulus,
was born.

■ Aeneas carrying his father Anchises – engraving from a
Greek vase

2 Nouns like puella; the six cases

Nouns like puella

In the same way that verbs in Latin have endings to show *who* is doing the verb, **nouns** in Latin have endings to show what part the noun is playing in the sentence.

As with verbs, nouns are divided up into groups, and these are called **DECLENSIONS**. Nouns of the 1st declension decline like puella:

Singular		
Nominative	puell-a	Girl (subject)
Vocative	puell-a	O girl!
Accusative	puell-am	Girl (object)
Genitive	puell-ae	Of a girl
Dative	puell-ae	To/for a girl
Ablative	puell-ā	By/with/from a girl
Plural		
Nominative	puell-ae	Girls (subject)
Vocative	puell-ae	O girls!
Accusative	puell-ās	Girls (object)
Genitive	puell-ārum	Of the girls
Dative	puell-īs	To/for the girls
Ablative	puell-īs	By/with/from the girls

The six cases

Nouns in Latin can be put into one of six **CASES** (nominative, vocative, accusative, genitive, dative or ablative) and can be singular or plural.

The **Nominative** case is used to show that the noun is the **subject** of the sentence, i.e. that the noun is the person or thing *doing the verb*.

The **Vocative** case is used for **addressing** the noun. Thus, if the noun were a name such as Cassia we would put her into the vocative case when addressing her: 'Cassia, how nice to see you!'

The **Accusative** case is used to show that the noun is the **object**, i.e. the person or thing *to which the verb is being done*.

The **Genitive** case is used for 'of'.

The **Dative** case is used for 'to' or 'for'.

The **Ablative** case is used for 'by', 'with' or 'from'. Note that the ablative singular ends in a long ā, which makes it sound different from the nominative and vocative singular, which both end in a short a.

> Latin has no definite or indefinite article. Thus puella = girl or *the* girl or *a* girl – depending on the context.

Exercise 2.1

Study the information above about puella. Notice how the ending of a Latin noun changes to reflect its meaning. All nouns of the 1st declension go like puella. We could thus write out the 1st declension nouns nauta = a sailor, and agricola = a farmer, as follows:

Nominative	naut-a	agricol-a
Vocative	naut-a	agricol-a
Accusative	naut-am	agricol-am
Genitive	naut-ae	agricol-ae
Dative	naut-ae	agricol-ae
Ablative	naut-ā	agricol-ā
Nominative	naut-ae	agricol-ae
Vocative	naut-ae	agricol-ae
Accusative	naut-ās	agricol-ās
Genitive	naut-ārum	agricol-ārum
Dative	naut-īs	agricol-īs
Ablative	naut-īs	agricol-īs

This is called writing out a noun in full. Write out the following nouns in full:

1 incola = inhabitant

2 rēgīna = queen

3 ancilla = slave-girl

4 poēta = poet

Exercise 2.2

Study the information above about the different meanings for each of the six cases. Then give the Latin for:

1 Of the farmer
2 To the sailor
3 Of a poet
4 By a spear
5 O slave-girls!

6 The farmers (subject)
7 The farmer (object)
8 For the sailors
9 O queen!
10 Of the poets

◯ Subjects and objects

The most important distinction which you must learn to make when dealing with nouns is that between subject and object.

1 The subject of a sentence is the person or thing *doing the verb*.
   E.g. The girl loves the farmer.
   In this example, the *girl* is the subject because she is doing the loving.
2 The object is the person or thing *having the verb done to him* or *her* or *it*. Thus in our example above, the *farmer* is the object because he is the one getting loved.

We can thus set out a simple English sentence using the initial **S** for subject, **V** for verb and **O** for object as follows:

S	V	O
The girl	loves	the farmer.
S	V	O
The farmers	watch	the girls.

We can do the same for Latin sentences. The subject goes in the **nominative case** and the object goes in the **accusative case**. The verb usually goes at the end.

S	O	V
puella	agricolam	amat.
S	O	V
agricolae	puellās	spectant.

Notice how the important thing in Latin is not the word order but the ENDINGS on the words. When working out which noun is the subject and which is the object, you need to look at the endings. The following table will help:

	Subject	Object
Singular	-a	-am
Plural	-ae	-ās

Exercise 2.3

Copy the following Latin sentences and look very carefully at the endings on the nouns. Write S over the subject, O over the object and V over the verb. Then translate them into English.

1 agricola puellam amat.

2 agricola nautās superat.

3 fēmina puellam amat.

4 nauta agricolam superat.

5 puellae agricolam amant.

6 fēmina aquam nōn parat.

7 agricolae viam parant.

8 nauta sagittās parat.

9 nautae īnsulam amant.

10 poētae deam nōn amant.

Exercise 2.4

Translate into English:

1 nautae incolās superant.

2 fēminae agricolās vocant.

3 dea īram nōn amat.

4 nautae pecūniam parant.

5 rēgīna ancillam vocat.

6 agricola terram spectat.

7 viam parant.

8 aquam spectāmus.

9 nautae īnsulam nōn spectant.

10 poēta sagittās nōn amat sed pugnat.

Exercise 2.5

Translate into English:

1 fēmina et puella ambulant.

2 agricolae et nautae pugnant.

3 fēmina patriam nōn amat.

4 nauta agricolam superat.

5 agricola puellās et poētās vocat.

6 egŏ aquam nōn amō.

7 tū pecūniam amās.

8 nōs sagittās et pecūniam parāmus.

9 vōs īnsulam spectātis.

10 poētae ancillās vocant.

Exercise 2.6

Translate into English:

1 agricolae viam nōn parant.
2 nautae agricolās spectant.
3 fēmina pecūniam parat.
4 ancilla et poēta agricolam spectant.
5 nōs viam aedificāmus.

6 vōs patriam et īnsulam amātis.
7 agricola poētam nōn amat.
8 egŏ hastās et sagittās parō.
9 tū viam spectās.
10 ancilla rēgīnam et poētam amat.

Subject 'in the verb'

The subject of a sentence is sometimes a noun (e.g. the sailors) and sometimes a pronoun (e.g. we). When the subject is a noun, we put that noun into the nominative case in Latin. When it is a pronoun, we say that the subject is 'in the verb', because the pronoun does not normally appear as a separate word (as it does in English); we only know who is doing the verb by looking at the ending.

If we wish to analyse the Latin for a sentence in which the subject is 'in the verb', there will be no noun to write S over, so we write V+S over the verb.

S	O	V		S	V	O
puella	agricolam	amat	=	The girl	loves	the farmer
	O	V+S		S	V	O
	agricolam	amat	=	She	loves	the farmer

> When a sentence has its subject 'in the verb', the first word we see in Latin will most probably be the object. When this happens, you must always translate the verb first, or you will end up muddling your subject with your object.

Exercise 2.7

Translate into English:

1 īnsulam spectant.
2 terram parat.
3 pecūniam nōn amāmus.
4 aquam parant.
5 sagittās nōn parātis.

6 incolās nōn superāmus.
7 viam parat.
8 patriam nōn amās.
9 fēminam superant.
10 deam nōn amant.

Exercise 2.8

Translate into English:

1 incolae īnsulam habitant.

2 agricolae terram nōn parant.

3 rēgīnam et pecūniam amat.

4 puellae aquam parant.

5 vōs hastās parātis.

6 incolās nōn spectāmus.

7 agricola viam parat.

8 deam nōn amātis.

9 incolae ancillam vocant.

10 aquam amat.

Exercise 2.9

Analyse the following sentences by writing S, V and O over the English words. Then complete the Latin nouns with the correct endings.

1 The farmer loves the girl.

agricol— puell— amat.

2 The girls love the queen.

puell— rēgīn— amant.

3 The sailors love the girls.

naut— puell— amant.

4 The girls love poets.

puell— poēt— amant.

5 The sailors overcome the farmers.

naut— agricol— superant.

6 The farmers overcome the sailors.

agricol— naut— superant.

7 The inhabitants prepare the arrows.

incol— sagitt— parant.

8 The goddess loves the poet.

de— poēt— amat.

9 He watches the sailors.

naut— spectat.

10 We overcome the inhabitants.

incol— superāmus.

◯ Verbs in the sentence

The verb in Latin very often, but not always, comes at the end of the sentence.

E.g. The girl loves the farmer = puella agricolam **amat**.

E.g. The farmers love the girl = agricolae puellam **amant**.

But notice, too, how the *verb ending* changes to reflect who is doing the verb. In the first example the subject was *the girl*, and so the verb ending was 3rd person singular (for 'she'). But in the second example the subject was *the farmers*, so the verb ending was 3rd person plural (for 'they').

Exercise 2.10

Put S over the subject, O over the object and V over the verb. Then add the correct endings to the Latin words.

1 The farmers love the women.

agricol— fēminās ama—.

2 The sailors love girls.

nautae puell— ama—.

3 The sailor watches the girl.

naut— puellam specta—.

4 The girl watches the sailor.

puella naut— specta—.

5 The sailors overcome the farmers.

nautae agricol— supera—.

6 The sailor overcomes the farmers.

naut— agricolās supera—.

7 The woman loves the goddess.

fēmina de— ama—.

8 The poet calls the farmer.

poēt— agricolam voca—.

9 We prepare the water.

aqu— parā—.

10 They prepare the way.

vi— para—.

Go further

Word order in Latin

As you have seen, Latin uses ENDINGS to show what the words in a sentence are doing. The subject *normally* comes first; the verb *normally* comes at the end.

But sometimes this normal word order is changed, usually to give a particular emphasis. If we really want to emphasise the verb, for example, which normally comes last, we put it first in the sentence. If we really want to emphasise the subject, which normally comes first, we put it last.

E.g.   agricolam superat puella = The *girl* is overcoming the farmer.

(We are emphasising the fact that it is the girl who is overcoming the farmer, not someone else.)

E.g.   cantant agricolae = The farmers are *singing*.

(We are emphasising the fact that the farmers are singing, rather than doing something else.)

It is thus really important that you learn to look at the endings of the Latin words, and not to rely on the word order to help you guess the meaning.

Exercise 2.11

Translate into English, paying attention to the endings, not the word order:

1 puella agricolam spectat.

2 agricolam puella spectat.

3 nautās agricola nōn amat.

4 agricola nautās nōn amat.

5 puellae agricolās spectant.

6 spectant agricolae puellās.

7 fēmina ancillās vocat.

8 ancillās nōn vocant.

9 cantant puella et fēmina.

10 puellae et fēminae cantant.

Exercise 2.12

Translate the following into English:

1 fēmina aquam parat.

2 aquam nōn parat.

3 agricolae patriam amant.

4 patriam nōs amāmus.

5 nautae sagittās parant.

6 vōs sagittās parātis.

7 ancillae nōn labōrant.

8 nōn labōrāmus.

9 agricola fēminam et ancillam spectat.

10 fēminam et ancillam spectant.

Exercise 2.13

Translate into Latin:

1 The sailors love the fatherland.

2 The farmer is working.

3 He is preparing the road.

4 The sailors are not fighting.

5 The farmers prepare a way.

6 She does not hurry.

7 They do not love water.

8 The girl is singing.

9 The woman is calling the slave-girls.

10 They are not singing.

Transitive and intransitive verbs

A sentence need not necessarily have a direct object. E.g. 'The girl is working' has a subject (*the girl*) and a verb (*is working*) but no object.

TRANSITIVE verbs (such as call, prepare, build, etc.) usually govern a direct object.

E.g. He prepares the water = aquam parat.

INTRANSITIVE verbs (such as work, hurry, walk, etc.) do not govern a direct object.

E.g. He is walking = ambulat.

The verb 'to be'

We have seen how regular verbs (like amō) behave. Now we are going to meet an irregular verb, sum = I am.

1st person singular	sum	I am
2nd person singular	es	You (sing.) are
3rd person singular	est	He, she or it is
1st person plural	sumus	We are
2nd person plural	estis	You (pl.) are
3rd person plural	sunt	They are

The verb 'to be' tells us, not what someone is *doing*, but what they are *being*.

E.g. Claudia fēmina est = Claudia is a woman.

E.g. Flāvia ancilla est = Flavia is a slave-girl.

E.g. nautae sumus = We are sailors.

Note that you cannot have an object after the verb 'to be'. The nouns both sides of the verb 'to be' go in the nominative case because they both refer to the subject.

Note, also, that names (such as Flāvia or Claudia) are nouns, and behave in the same way as other nouns, changing their endings to show whether they are the subject or the object.

E.g. Flāvia Claudiam spectat = Flavia watches Claudia.

Exercise 2.14

Translate into English:

1 agricola sum.
2 nauta es.
3 Flāvia ancilla est.
4 agricolae sumus.
5 nautae estis.

6 Flāvia et Iulia ancillae sunt.
7 Cassia fēmina est.
8 Flāvia ancilla nōn est.
9 Claudia et Sulpicia puellae sunt.
10 Flāvia et Iulia agricolae nōn sunt.

Exercise 2.15

Translate into Latin:

1 He is a poet.
2 She is a slave-girl.
3 Cassia is a woman.
4 I am a farmer.
5 We are sailors.

6 You (pl.) are not farmers.
7 They are not poets.
8 He is a sailor.
9 Cassia and Flavia are slave-girls.
10 You (sing.) are a sailor.

Exercise 2.16

Translate into English:

1 ancilla est.
2 nautae sumus.
3 rēgīna dea nōn est.
4 incola poēta nōn est.
5 nōs agricolae sumus.

6 vōs ancillae estis.
7 tū poēta es.
8 egǒ deam spectō et amō.
9 incola agricola nōn est.
10 Flāvia ancilla est.

Exercise 2.17

Translate into Latin:

1 We love the poets.
2 The sailor loves water.
3 They overcome the country.
4 The woman loves water.
5 He does not overcome the sailor.

6 They call the farmer.
7 I do not like the poet.
8 They watch the queen.
9 You (pl.) are building a road.
10 She does not call the slave-girl.

Copy and complete the table below to show the connection between English and Latin words. The first one has been done for you.

English word	Latin word	Meaning of Latin word
amorous	amō	I love
1 feminine		
2 aquatic		
3 insular		
4 laborious		
5 navigate		

Translating from Latin: golden rules

For the Romans, speaking and writing in Latin was very simple. They put the subject in the nominative case, the object in the accusative case, and the verb at the end with the correct ending. For us, translating *out of* Latin can be a touch tricky at first, but if you follow a few golden rules, you should be fine:

1 **Always look at the verb first.**
   The verb tells us what is happening, and who is doing it. Look at the ending of the verb to see which person it is (I, you, he, etc.). The verb is often *but not always* at the end of the sentence.

2 **Look for a noun in the nominative case.**
   Unless the subject is 'in the verb' there will be a noun in the nominative case. If the verb is singular (he, she or it), this noun will be nominative singular. If the verb is plural (they) the noun will be nominative plural (or two or more nouns in the nominative joined by 'and').

3 **Look for a noun in the accusative case.**
   The object, if there is one, will be in the accusative case. As a general rule you should *never translate an accusative case before the verb*. If you do, you will probably have muddled your subject with your object.

It will help if you analyse the sentence by writing V over the verb, S over the subject, and O over the object. Remember, if the subject is 'in the verb', write V+S over the verb. Note that it is the *endings*, not the word order, which shows whether a noun is the subject or object.

	S	O	V
E.g.	puella	agricolam	amat

and

	O	S	V
	agricolam	puella	amat

both mean *the girl loves the farmer*.

Exercise 2.19

Translate into English:

1 ancillae fēminās nōn amant.

2 fēminās nōn amant.

3 rēgīna deam spectat.

4 deam spectat.

5 nōs agricolam spectāmus.

6 vōs ancillās vocātis.

7 pecūniam poēta spectat.

8 viam aedificant et terram parant.

9 ancillae nōn festīnant.

10 agricolam spectātis.

Nouns in the vocabulary

When we list nouns in the vocabulary, we give three pieces of information: the genitive singular ending, the gender and the meaning. All three must be learnt.

The genitive singular ending for nouns of the 1st declension is -ae, and so all 1st declension nouns will appear in the vocabulary with the letters -ae after them, e.g. agricola, -ae. Alternatively, the genitive singular may sometimes be written in full, e.g. agricola, agricolae.

The gender of a noun may be masculine (m.), feminine (f.), common (c.) or neuter (n.). *Common* means that the noun can be either masculine or feminine. *Neuter* is the Latin for neither, and means simply that the noun is neither masculine nor feminine (rather like the English 'it'). We will meet some neuter nouns in Chapter 4.

Vocabulary 2

Latin	English
agricola, -ae, m.	farmer
ancilla, -ae, f.	slave-girl
aqua, -ae, f.	water
dea, -ae, f.	goddess
fēmina, -ae, f.	woman
fīlia, -ae, f.	daughter
hasta, -ae, f.	spear
incola, -ae, c.	inhabitant
īnsula, -ae, f.	island
īra, -ae, f.	anger
nauta, -ae, m.	sailor
patria, -ae, f.	country, fatherland
poēta, -ae, m.	poet
puella, -ae, f.	girl
rēgīna, -ae, f.	queen
sagitta, -ae, f.	arrow
terra, -ae, f.	land, ground
via, -ae, f.	road, street, way
sum	I am

Romulus and Remus

Aeneas's son Ascanius left Lavinium to build his own city, Alba Longa. Many generations later the king of Alba Longa, Proca, died leaving two sons, Numitor and Amulius. The younger son, Amulius, seized the throne from Numitor and locked up his brother's daughter, Rhea Silvia, forcing her to become a Vestal Virgin. Vestal Virgins were not allowed to marry.

According to the legend, the god Mars took pity on Rhea Silvia and fell in love with her. Nine months later twin boys, Romulus and Remus, were born, but the babies were immediately discovered and thrown into the River Tiber.

However, it so happened that the river was flooded at the time and when the flood subsided, Romulus and Remus were washed up on the river bank where they were found by a she-wolf. Legend has it

This topic is part of the Non-Linguistic Studies section of the ISEB syllabus.

that the twins were suckled by the she-wolf, and a famous bronze statue in Rome commemorates this tradition (see below). A few days later the boys were found in the she-wolf's cave by a shepherd called Faustulus, who brought the boys up as his own and trained them to be shepherds.

Some years later, the twins became involved in a dispute between shepherds working for King Amulius and those working for their grandfather, Numitor. Some of Numitor's men dragged Remus before Numitor, accusing him of having stolen some sheep. Numitor thought he recognised the boy, and when Romulus arrived to rescue his brother, and Numitor saw the twins together, he knew that these were his long lost grandsons. He told the twins the story of their birth, and how he himself had been dispossessed by his wicked younger brother. Romulus and Remus were outraged and together they drove Amulius from the kingdom and restored Numitor to the throne.

Exercise 2.20

Find out what you can about the birth of Romulus and Remus.

(a) Tell the story of how Romulus and Remus came to be brought up by a shepherd.

(b) To what extent do you think the Romans believed every detail of the story?

■ Romulus and Remus feeding from the she-wolf

3 The imperfect tense; using all the cases

The imperfect tense

So far you have met amō and sum in the present tense, but we now need to learn how verbs work in the imperfect tense. The imperfect tense refers to a continuous action in the past. Thus, if we wish to know what *was happening* or *happened* in the past, we use the imperfect tense. To form the imperfect tense of amō, all we do is add a different set of endings to the present stem (amā-):

amā-bam	I was loving, loved
amā-bās	You (sing.) were loving, loved
amā-bat	He, she, it was loving, loved
amā-bāmus	We were loving, loved
amā-bātis	You (pl.) were loving, loved
amā-bant	They were loving, loved

Exercise 3.1

Translate into English:

1 clāmābat.
2 habitābāmus.
3 labōrābant.
4 vocābātis.
5 festīnābam.
6 aedificābās.
7 nāvigābat.
8 cantābant.
9 superābātis.
10 spectābant.

Exercise 3.2

Translate into Latin:

1 I was building.
2 They were working.
3 You (sing.) were sailing.
4 He built.
5 She was singing.
6 You (pl.) were hurrying.
7 We hurried.
8 We were calling.
9 You (pl.) called.
10 They were singing.

Exercise 3.3

Translate into English:

1 agricolae viam parābant.

2 ancillae aquam spectābant.

3 incolae deam amābant.

4 vōs nautās vocābātis.

5 egŏ nōn festīnābam.

6 agricolae et nautae pugnābant.

7 nauta nōn nāvigābat.

8 cantābant et clāmābant.

9 agricolae nautās superābant.

10 fēminae rēgīnam spectābant.

Imperfect of sum

The imperfect tense of sum goes as follows:

eram	I was
erās	You (sing.) were
erat	He, she, it was
erāmus	We were
erātis	You (pl.) were
erant	They were

Exercise 3.4

Translate into English:

1 Cassia ancilla erat.

2 Iūlia et Sulpicia fēminae erant.

3 tū agricola erās.

4 nōs nautae erāmus.

5 egŏ poēta eram.

6 ancillae erāmus.

7 poēta fēmina erat.

8 agricola erat; labōrābat.

9 poētae nōn erātis.

10 nautae erant et nāvigābānt.

Exercise 3.5

Translate into English. Note that these are a mixture of present and imperfect tenses, so look carefully at the endings:

1 aedificant.

2 festīnābant.

3 nōn pugnābāmus.

4 erātis.

5 egŏ cantābam sed tū labōrābās.

6 erant.

7 pugnābat et superābat.

8 spectātis.

9 erās.

10 nāvigābat.

Exercise 3.6

Translate into Latin:

1 He builds.
2 They were fighting.
3 We were.
4 You (pl.) sailed.
5 They were not watching.

6 He does not fight.
7 You (sing.) loved.
8 We were not watching.
9 She was.
10 I was walking.

Exercise 3.7

Translate into English:

1 fēmina patriam nōn amābat.
2 incolae deam amābant.
3 agricolae et nautae pugnābant.
4 rēgīna patriam habitābat.
5 agricolae terram parābant.

6 poēta erat.
7 fēmina fīliam spectābat.
8 hastās parābāmus.
9 sagittās et hastās incolae parābant.
10 nauta nōn nāvigābat.

The vocative and genitive cases

So far you have learnt to write out 1st declension nouns in full, and to write and translate sentences involving subjects (in the nominative case) and objects (in the accusative case). We now need to look at how the other cases are used.

Vocative case

When addressing a noun, we put the noun we are addressing into the vocative case.

E.g. 'O sailors, you love the island' = 'īnsulam, **nautae**, amātis.'

Notice how the vocative in Latin is normally inserted into the middle of the sentence, between commas, or placed at the end, rather than coming at the beginning as it does in English. Note also that the word 'O' may be used, in both English and Latin, but is not necessary in either language.

Exercise 3.8

Translate into English:

1 'patriam amās, fēmina.'

2 'patriam, incolae, amātis.'

3 'nōn pugnātis, agricolae et nautae.'

4 'egŏ, ō rēgīna, patriam habitābam.'

5 'nōs, agricolae, terram parābāmus.'

6 'poēta, ō Cassia, eram.'

7 'fīliam, fēmina, nōn laudābās.'

8 'hastās, dea, parābās.'

9 'sagittās, agricola, parābam.'

10 'aquam, nauta, nōn amābās.'

Genitive case

The genitive case is used to express possession. In English we either use the word 'of' or else we use an apostrophe. In Latin, the 'possessor' (i.e. the noun doing the possessing) is put into the genitive case.

E.g. *the farmer's* money (or the money *of the farmer*) = pecūnia **agricolae**

E.g. *the farmers'* money (or the money *of the farmers*) = pecūnia **agricolārum**

Care needs to be taken with the apostrophe in English. Remember that, with most nouns, if the apostrophe comes before the s (e.g. farmer's), the possessor is singular; if it comes after the s (e.g. farmers') it is plural. If in any doubt, take out the apostrophe and put in the word 'of'.

E.g. the *girl's* money = the money *of the girl*.

E.g. the *girls'* money = the money *of the girls*.

Extra care needs to be taken with English nouns which don't form their plural by adding 's'.

E.g. the *woman's* money = the money *of the woman* (singular);

E.g. the *women's* money = the money *of the women* (plural).

Exercise 3.9

Translate into English:

1 fīliam agricolae amās.

2 incola rēgīnam īnsulae amat.

3 fīliam poētae vocābās.

4 rēgīna incolās īnsulārum amat.

5 incolae hastās agricolārum parābant.

6 fīliae poētae cantābant.

7 tū fīliās rēgīnae spectābās.

8 incolās patriae amās.

9 vōs fīliae agricolae estis.

10 pecūniam rēgīnae spectābant.

Exercise 3.10

Translate into Latin:

1 Of the farmer

2 Of the farmers

3 Of the island

4 Of the islands

5 Of the goddess

6 The money of the sailor

7 The sailor's money

8 I love the daughter of the queen.

9 We love the queen's daughter.

10 The slave-girls were not preparing the queen's water.

Exercise 3.11

Translate into English:

1 'fīliam agricolae, ancilla, spectābās.'

2 rēgīnam īnsulae amās.

3 agricola fīliās poētae vocābat.

4 rēgīnam īnsulārum amābat.

5 īram rēgīnae nōn amāmus.

6 fīlia poētae cantābat.

7 egŏ fīliam rēgīnae spectābam.

8 'patriam amō, rēgīna.'

9 nōs ancillās rēgīnae laudābāmus.

10 pecūniam agricolae spectābās.

Exercise 3.12

Translate into Latin:

1 The slave-girl watches the daughter of the farmer.

2 The slave-girl's daughter watches the farmer.

3 We were overcoming the inhabitants of the island.

4 The inhabitants of the island were fighting.

5 'O queen, we love the fatherland!'

6 The farmer was preparing the woman's money.

7 The sailor is preparing the women's money.

8 I love the queen of the island.

9 They were calling the queen's daughter.

10 The girls were watching the poet's daughters.

Go further

The genitive in Latin may come *before* or *after* the other noun.

E.g. *The farmer's* money = pecūnia **agricolae**

OR

agricolae pecūnia.

E.g. The money *of the farmers* = pecūnia **agricolārum**

OR

agricolārum pecūnia.

The dative and ablative cases

Dative case

The dative case is used to translate 'to' or 'for'.

E.g. The farmer sings *to the girls* = agricola **puellīs** cantat.

Exercise 3.13

Translate into Latin, using the dative case:

1 To the farmer
2 To the slave-girl
3 To the poets
4 For the queen
5 For the goddess
6 To the inhabitant
7 For the inhabitants
8 For the daughter
9 To the women
10 For the girls

Ablative case

The ablative case is used for the instrument *by means of which* we do something. It is often translated by the words *by* or *with*.

E.g. The farmer overcomes the sailor *with arrows* = agricola nautam **sagittīs** superat.

Exercise 3.14

Translate into Latin, using the ablative case:

1 With an arrow

2 With a spear

3 With water

4 With arrows

5 With spears

6 With spears and arrows

7 With an arrow and a spear

8 He overcame the farmer with a spear.

9 They overcame the inhabitants with arrows.

10 I was not fighting with a spear.

Exercise 3.15

Translate into English:

1 nauta aquam fēminae nōn dăbat.

2 poēta incolīs nōn cantābat.

3 rēgīna pecūniam agricolīs dat.

4 ancilla aquam puellae parat.

5 nautae agricolam sagittā necant.

6 incolae sagittīs et hastīs pugnābant.

7 hastam rēgīnae nōn parābam.

8 ancillīs agricolārum cantābāmus.

9 poētīs aquam parābat.

10 'pecūniam agricolae, rēgīna, nōn dăbās.'

Go further

The verb dō, dăre = I give

Note that, unlike other 1st conjugation verbs, the verb dō has a short ă in its present stem (although it reverts to a long ā in the 2nd person singular of the present tense). Its tenses should be pronounced as shown in the table opposite:

3 The imperfect tense: using all the cases

dō	dăbam
dās	dăbās
dat	dăbat
dămus	dăbāmus
dătis	dăbātis
dant	dăbant

Exercise 3.16

Translate into Latin:

1 The sailor prepares water for the queen.

2 You (sing.) were singing to the woman.

3 We were preparing spears and arrows for the inhabitants.

4 He was giving a spear to the farmer.

5 They kill the sailors with spears.

6 I was giving money to the slave-girl.

7 They were preparing water for the women.

8 You (pl.) love the farmer's daughter.

9 The farmer's daughter was singing to the queen.

10 They were preparing a way for the inhabitants.

Go further

Coping with all the cases

We have already seen that some cases in Latin use the same endings. Thus -ae can be genitive singular, dative singular, nominative plural or vocative plural. When we translate longer sentences this can become a problem.

For example, study the following sentence:

incolae terrae viam agricolae aedificant.

The ending -ae occurs three times in this sentence, so how can we tell which case each one is supposed to be? We know the verb is aedificant and the subject would *normally* be the first word in the sentence. As the first word (incolae) looks as if it is in the nominative plural, we can assume that it is the subject. The other words then fall into place, and we get: 'The inhabitants of the land build a way for the farmer.' But the truth is, the sentence could mean other things (for example, it could mean 'The farmers build a way for the inhabitant of the land'), and sometimes you simply have to use the context to guide you as to what it means.

Translate into English:

1 puella fēminīs cantābat.

2 agricolae viam incolīs aedificābant.

3 incolae īnsulae deam amābant.

4 'agricolās superābātis, nautae!'

5 incolae aquam agricolīs parābant.

6 nautae incolam sagittīs superābant.

7 'viās et terram, agricolae, incolīs parābātis.'

8 patriam poētārum et agricolārum nōn amant.

9 pecūniam agricolae dabāmus.

10 pecūniam agricolae ancillīs dabās.

Exercise 3.18

Study the information above about the use of all the cases. Before attempting to translate into Latin, it is a good idea to analyse each sentence, working out which cases you will need. S, V and O will appear as normal, but the extra cases can be added as follows:

S	V	O	Gen.
The farmer	loves	the land	of the inhabitants
S	V	O	Abl.
The sailor	overcomes	the farmer	with an arrow

Analyse the following sentences and then translate into Latin:

1 The sailor loves the daughter of the farmer.

2 The inhabitants killed the sailors with arrows.

3 We were fighting with spears and arrows.

4 They were preparing a road for the inhabitants.

5 He prepared water for the woman.

6 'O girls, the farmers are singing to the women.'

7 The arrows of the inhabitants overcome the sailors.

8 They were preparing water for the women.

9 'O farmers, you overcome the country with arrows.'

10 'O sailors, you were overcoming the inhabitants.'

Exercise 3.19

Analyse and translate the following:

1 puella ancillās agricolae nōn amābat.

2 agricola fīliam nōn amābat.

3 fēmina aquam agricolīs parābat.

4 puella sagittās agricolīs nōn parābat.

5 'fēminās, agricolae, sagittīs nōn superābātis.'

6 'agricola, puellae, fēminās nōn superābat.'

7 incolae agricolās sagittīs superābant.

8 nautae incolās īnsulae superābant.

9 nōs pecūniam agricolae dabāmus.

10 egŏ fīliae rēgīnae nōn cantō.

Exercise 3.20

Translate the following, giving all alternative meanings where appropriate:

1 agricolae

2 sagittā

3 puellīs

4 terrārum

5 aquā

6 ancillārum

7 sagittīs

8 viae

9 pecūniam

10 īra

Prepositions

Prepositions are words placed before a noun which give information about that noun. E.g. *under* the water, *on* the road, *towards* the farmers.

In Latin the preposition 'governs' (i.e. is followed by) a particular case, either the accusative or the ablative. Some prepositions govern the accusative, some govern the ablative. When you learn the preposition, you have to learn which case it governs or is followed by.

In this course you need to learn eleven prepositions, six followed by the accusative and five followed by the ablative:

ad + acc.	to, towards	ā/ab + abl.	by, from
contrā + acc.	against	cum + abl.	with
in + acc.	into, on to	dē + abl.	down from, concerning
per + acc.	through	ē/ex + abl.	out of
prope + acc.	near	in + abl.	in, on
trāns + acc.	across		

Using these prepositions, we can write:

Towards the island = ad īnsulam

With the slave-girls = cum ancillīs

Through the water = per aquam

Concerning the women = dē fēminīs

1 Particular care needs to be taken with the Latin preposition in. When it is followed by the accusative it means *into* or *on to*, but when it is followed by the ablative it means *in* or *on*.
   E.g. in aquam = into the water.
   E.g. in aquā = in the water.
2 ad = 'to', in the sense of 'towards' (e.g. he sails to the island, i.e. *towards* the island). This should not be confused with the normal use of the dative case (meaning 'to').
3 The preposition ā becomes ab if the next word begins with a vowel or h.
   E.g. ā viā, but ab aquā.
4 The preposition cum = 'with', in the sense of 'together with' (e.g. he walks with the woman, i.e. *together with* the woman). This should not be confused with the normal use of the ablative for 'with' meaning 'by means of' (e.g. he killed the farmer *with* an arrow, i.e. *by means of* an arrow).
5 The preposition ē becomes ex before a vowel or h.
   E.g. ē patriā but ex aquā.

Exercise 3.21

Translate into English:

1 in viā
2 contrā agricolās
3 in viam
4 ā patriā
5 cum agricolā
6 in aquam
7 dē deā
8 per viās
9 prope aquam
10 ad īnsulam
11 ā terrā
12 prope viam
13 in aquā
14 in terram
15 contrā incolās
16 dē īrā
17 ex īnsulā
18 cum ancillīs
19 ē terrā
20 trāns aquam

Exercise 3.22

Translate into Latin:

1 Towards the island
2 Through the streets
3 Into the water
4 Against the inhabitants
5 In the water
6 With the women
7 Near the farmer
8 Concerning the poet
9 Out of the country
10 Through the water
11 With the poet
12 Across the land
13 Out of the water
14 Near the women
15 Towards the slave-girls
16 With the queen
17 Against the sailors
18 In the island
19 On the island
20 Through the water

Exercise 3.23

When translating sentences containing prepositions, it is a good idea when analysing to bracket prepositions together with the nouns they govern, as in the first few shown below. Translate into English:

1 nauta [ā patriā] nāvigābat.
2 [ad īnsulam] nōn festīnābat.
3 agricolae [cum incolīs] pugnant.
4 agricolae per viās ambulābant.
5 ad aquam nōn festīnābant.
6 nautae cum agricolīs pugnābant.
7 per viās patriae ambulābant.
8 prope aquam rēgīna cantābat.
9 pecūniam ad rēgīnam portābant.
10 poētae incolīs nōn cantābant.

Exercise 3.24

Translate into Latin:

1 He walks towards the queen.

2 They do not hurry into the street.

3 He sails towards the islands.

4 He is shouting about the money.

5 I am not fighting with the sailors.

6 The farmer was working in the street.

7 The girls were walking with the queen.

8 I was not asking about the money.

9 He kills farmers with a spear.

10 He gives money to the woman.

Go further

Clauses

A clause is a grammatical unit that contains a verb. Most of the sentences you have translated so far have been single clauses, but where a sentence contains more than one clause, you simply translate the first clause first, and then move on to the next. Sentences like this will be easy to spot because there will be more than one verb, with the first clause linked to the second by a conjunction (e.g. et or sed).

E.g. nautae ad īnsulam nāvigābant et incolās superābant.

> The sailors were sailing to the island and were overcoming the inhabitants.

Exercise 3.25

Translate the following into English. Make sure that, in each sentence, you deal with the first clause first, before moving on to the second one.

1 agricolae terram parābant et viam aedificābant.

2 incolae agricolās spectābant et labōrābant.

3 fēminae nōn labōrant sed agricolīs cantant.

4 puellae aquam nōn parābant sed agricolās spectābant.

5 agricolae nōn labōrābant sed in aquam festīnābant.

6 egŏ ad rēgīnam festīnābam sed tū prope aquam labōrābās.

7 poēta rēgīnae cantābat sed rēgīna pecūniam parābat.

8 nautae trāns aquam nāvigābant et agricolae viam aedificābant.

9 fīliam rēgīnae nōn amābat; ancillam amābat.

10 vos sagittās incolārum parābātis et cum nautīs pugnābātis.

Exercise 3.26

Copy and complete the blanks in the following table to show the connection between English and Latin words. The first one has been done for you.

	English word	Latin word	Meaning of Latin word
	amorous	amō	I love
1	insulate		
2	laudable		
3	habitation		
4	portable		
5	transatlantic		
6		contrā	
7		vocant	
8		narrat	
9		nauta	
10		patria	

Vocabulary 3

Latin	English
Prepositions	
ad + acc.	to, towards
contrā + acc.	against
in + acc.	into, on to
per + acc.	through
prope + acc.	near
trāns + acc.	across
ā/ab + abl.	by, from
cum + abl.	with
dē + abl.	down from, concerning
ē/ex + abl.	out of
in + abl.	in, on
Verbs	
dō	I give
habitō	I live (in)
intrō	I enter
laudō	I praise
necō	I kill
oppugnō	I attack
portō	I carry
rogō	I ask
stō	I stand

The foundation of Rome

After Romulus and Remus had driven the wicked king Amulius from the throne and put their old grandfather, Numitor, in his place, the twins felt they needed a kingdom of their own. They set off to the place where Faustulus had first found them in the she-wolf's cave. This was a suitable place to build a new city, being a level plain, surrounded by seven hills. But they couldn't decide who should be the king of the new city.

This topic is part of the Non-Linguistic Studies section of the ISEB syllabus.

In the ancient world, it was common to use **augury** to find answers to questions such as this. Augury is a form of fortune-telling, and relies on signs or omens from the natural world to provide answers to questions or problems. Observing the behaviour of birds was one popular form of augury.

Deciding that they would rely on augury to resolve the matter, Romulus climbed the Palatine Hill and Remus climbed the Aventine. There they waited to see what the birds would tell them. After a while, Remus saw six vultures, flying across the sky above him. Taking this to be a good omen, he ran down the hill and up the Palatine to tell his brother. However, when he got there Romulus said that *he* had seen twelve vultures, and so it was decided that the city should be called Rome after its first king, Romulus.

A few days later, Remus, unhappy with the outcome, mocked his brother by jumping over a low wall which was in the process of being built around the new city. His brother flew into a rage and killed Remus with the words 'thus perish anyone who jumps over my walls!'

Exercise 3.27

(a) Tell the story of the foundation of Rome.

(b) How much of the story do you think is true, and how much pure legend?

■ Dedication to Romulus inscribed on stone

The 2nd conjugation; 2nd declension nouns

○ Verbs of the 2nd conjugation: moneō

The regular verbs you have met so far have been 1st conjugation, going like amō. The next type of verb to learn belongs to the 2nd conjugation and goes like moneō = I warn or advise.

Moneō uses exactly the same endings as amō, but instead of having a present stem ending in -ā it has one ending in -ē.

moneō = I warn / advise			
Present Tense		**Imperfect Tense**	
mone-ō	I warn	monē-bam	I was warning
monē-s	You (sing.) warn	monē-bās	You (sing.) were warning
mone-t	He, she, it warns	monē-bat	He, she, it was warning
monē-mus	We warn	monē-bāmus	We were warning
monē-tis	You (pl.) warn	monē-bātis	You (pl.) were warning
mone-nt	They warn	monē-bant	They were warning

Exercise 4.1

Make a note of the 2nd conjugation verbs in the vocabulary at the end of the chapter. Then translate into English:

1 timēbat.

2 movēbant.

3 nōn rīdētis.

4 monēbat.

5 habet.

6 videt.

7 habent.

8 timētis.

9 vidēbātis.

10 rīdēmus.

11 rīdēbant.

12 monēbātis.

13 habētis.

14 timent.

15 vidēbās.

16 timēbant.

17 movētis.

18 nōn movēbātis.

19 rīdēbat.

20 habent.

Exercise 4.2

Using the vocabulary in Vocabulary 4 below, translate into Latin:

1 He was warning.

2 They see.

3 We fear.

4 She was seeing.

5 You (pl.) do not fear.

6 They advise.

7 They were laughing.

8 He feared.

9 You (sing.) moved.

10 We do not fear

11 They were moving.

12 I was fearing.

13 You (pl.) do not have.

14 I fear.

15 They were seeing.

16 You (sing.) do not see.

17 He was laughing and singing.

18 They were advising.

19 She laughs.

20 We do not see.

The present infinitive

Verbs in Latin have **principal parts**. These are the four most important parts of the verb and are used to classify the verbs into their conjugations.

The first principal part of a verb is the one we use when referring to it, such as amō or moneō or sum.

The second principal part is the **present infinitive**, and for regular verbs this always ends in -re.

> amāre = to love
>
> monēre = to warn

1st conjugation verbs like amō always have a present infinitive ending in -āre and 2nd conjugation verbs like moneō always have a present infinitive ending in -ēre.

E.g.   ambulāre = to walk

vocāre = to call

timēre = to fear, to be afraid

vidēre = to see

The 2nd conjugation; 2nd declension nouns

4

The present infinitive of the irregular verb sum is, as one might expect, irregular:

> esse = to be

And we have seen that, unlike other 1st conjugation verbs, the present infinitive of dō = I give has a short a: dăre.

Exercise 4.3

Study the information above about the present infinitive. Translate the following:

1 vocāre.

2 habēre.

3 rogāre.

4 rīdēre.

5 movēre.

6 laudāre.

7 esse.

8 amat pugnāre.

9 timet spectāre.

10 nōn timet intrāre.

11 ambulāre.

12 clāmāre.

13 habēre.

14 labōrāre.

15 monēre.

16 vidēre.

17 dăre.

18 timēre.

19 nāvigāre.

20 amō labōrāre.

Exercise 4.4

Translate into Latin:

1 To sail

2 To work

3 To see

4 To laugh

5 To be

6 To give

7 To have

8 To overcome

9 To love

10 To like

11 To prepare

12 To fear

13 To fight

14 To warn

15 To advise

16 They love to give.

17 I love to fight.

18 We love to sing.

19 They love to work.

20 He is afraid to kill.

Exercise 4.5

Translate into English:

1 ancilla cantāre amat.

2 pecūniam habēre amāmus.

3 cum agricolā pugnāre amābātis.

4 rēgīnam vocāre nōn amat.

5 nautae ad īnsulam nāvigāre amant.

6 agricolae cum fēminīs labōrāre amābant.

7 pugnāre cum nautīs amat.

8 poētae cantāre et rīdēre amant.

9 nautae nāvigāre nōn amābant.

10 nōs rēgīnae cantāre amāmus.

Exercise 4.6

Translate into English:

1 ancillae aquam movent.

2 nōs pecūniam nōn habēmus.

3 vōs cum agricolā rīdēbātis.

4 puellae rēgīnam nōn timent.

5 nautae patriam vidēbant.

6 incolae et nautae pugnābant.

7 rēgīna ancillam monēbat.

8 pōēta cantābat et rīdēbat.

9 nautae sagittās nōn habēbant.

10 fīlia rēgīnae rīdēre amat.

2nd declension nouns: dominus

All the nouns you have met so far have been 1st declension nouns like puella. It is now time to meet the 2nd declension.

2nd declension nouns in -us go like dominus = a lord, or master. They are almost always masculine.

4   *The 2nd conjugation; 2nd declension nouns*

dominus, dominī, m. = lord, master		
Nom.	domin-us	Lord (subject)
Voc.	domin-e	O lord (addressing)
Acc.	domin-um	Lord (object)
Gen.	domin-ī	Of a lord
Dat.	domin-ō	To, for a lord
Abl.	domin-ō	By, with or from a lord
Nom.	domin-ī	Lords (subject)
Voc.	domin-ī	O lords (addressing)
Acc.	domin-ōs	Lords (object)
Gen.	domin-ōrum	Of the lords
Dat.	domin-īs	To, for the lords
Abl.	domin-īs	By, with or from the lords

Go further

Stems and endings

2nd declension nouns always have a genitive singular ending in -ī. The stem of a noun can be found by looking at the genitive singular and chopping off the ending. Thus the genitive singular of dominus is dominī. If we take off the -ī ending we are left with the stem domin-.

Sometimes care needs to be taken to get the correct stem. For example the Latin for a sword is gladius, which has the genitive singular gladiī (with two 'i's). If we take off the -ī ending from this, we are left with gladi-. Where a noun has a stem ending in -i, be aware that this will usually lead to your getting two 'i's together (e.g. gladiī and gladiīs).

In this chapter you have had to cope with being told that not all verbs go like amō and not all nouns go like puella. The 2nd conjugation (moneō) and the 2nd declension (dominus) have crept up to make life complicated.

From now on, then, when working with nouns and verbs, make sure you know which sort they are before trying to add endings to them. Until further notice, nouns ending in -a must go like puella; nouns in -us go like dominus.

Exercise 4.7

Study the information above about 2nd declension nouns like dominus. Notice how, just as with puella, the endings are added to the noun stem. Write out in full the following nouns.

1 cibus, cibī, m. = food

2 amīcus, amīcī, m. = friend

3 equus, equī, m. = horse

4 mūrus, mūrī, m. = wall

5 servus, servī, m. = slave

Exercise 4.8

Translate into English:

1 ad mūrum

2 ab īnsulā

3 cum dominō

4 per aquam

5 in aquā

6 nūntiōrum

7 cum nūntiīs

8 'serve!'

9 prope amīcum

10 in aquam

Exercise 4.9

Give the Latin for, using prepositions where necessary:

1 Of the lord

2 Near the horse

3 For the messenger

4 With the lord

5 Towards the wall

6 Of the messengers

7 With the masters

8 Across the wall

9 'O messengers'

10 Towards the friends

Exercise 4.10

Translate into English:

1 ad īnsulam

2 ā mūrō

3 cum dominīs

4 per viam

5 in viā

6 prope mūrum

7 cum amīcīs

8 trāns mūrōs

9 prope equum

10 dē mūrō

Exercise 4.11

Translate into English:

1 amīcus cibum amat.

2 nūntius mūrum spectat.

3 ancilla dominum gladiō necat.

4 servus per viās festīnābat.

5 servī fīliam dominī nōn amant.

6 cibum vidēbāmus.

7 ancillae cum servīs rīdēbant.

8 puerī trāns mūrum spectant.

9 agricolae prope equum stant.

10 gladiīs et hastīs pugnābātis.

Exercise 4.12

Translate into Latin. Some of the nouns are 1st declension, some are 2nd declension. Some of the verbs are 1st conjugation, some are 2nd conjugation. Remember to use the correct endings with the different declensions and conjugations.

1 The slaves fear the master.

2 The women saw the slaves.

3 The messenger calls the inhabitants.

4 The farmer moves the horses.

5 The friends were looking at the food.

6 We have food and water.

7 He was giving a sword to the queen.

8 The master prepares the food for the inhabitants.

9 The slaves prepared the water for the master.

10 The messengers were singing to the slave.

Nouns like bellum

The other main type of 2nd declension noun goes like bellum = war. Nouns that end in -um go like bellum and are neuter, i.e. neither masculine nor feminine.

bellum, bell-ī, n. = war		
Nom.	bell-um	War (subject)
Voc.	bell-um	O war (addressing)
Acc.	bell-um	War (object)
Gen.	bell-ī	Of a war
Dat.	bell-ō	To, for a war
Abl.	bell-ō	By, with or from a war
Nom.	bell-a	Wars (subject)
Voc.	bell-a	O wars (addressing)
Acc.	bell-a	Wars (object)
Gen.	bell-ōrum	Of the wars
Dat.	bell-īs	To, for the wars
Abl.	bell-īs	By, with or from the wars

Exercise 4.13

Study the information above about nouns like bellum. Then write out the following nouns in full.

1 verbum, verbī, n. = word

2 oppidum, oppidī, n. = town

3 scūtum, scūtī, n. = shield

4 perīculum, perīculī, n. = danger

Exercise 4.14

Translate into English:

1 agricola scūtum habet.

2 agricolae scūta habent.

3 verbum timeō.

4 verba timēbam.

5 ancilla perīcula timet.

6 dominus templum aedificat.

7 dominus templa aedificat.

8 verba dominī timēmus.

9 nauta scūtum nōn habēbat.

10 incola scūta ad oppida portābat.

Exercise 4.15

Translate into Latin:

1 We see a temple.

2 You (pl.) have shields.

3 They fear the dangers.

4 The master has a shield.

5 The woman loves the town.

6 In the town.

7 Into the town.

8 Towards the town.

9 Towards the towns.

10 The farmers walk towards the temple.

Working with neuters

The main difficulty with neuter nouns is that there is no difference between their nominative, vocative and accusative cases, so working out whether a noun is the subject or the object is that much more difficult. (It is also possible to muddle the -a (plural) endings of a neuter noun with the -a (singular) endings of a 1st declension noun like puella, but only if you haven't learnt your vocabulary properly.)

So how do we cope then? We see the ending -um but can no longer be sure that this is an accusative singular ending (as it would be for dominus type nouns). Again, we fall back on common sense and, of course, obeying the rules of translation carefully.

```
    ?          V
```

E.g. bellum nōn amat = he does not love the war

(**Common sense:** bellum could have been nominative, but 'the war does not love' makes no sense!)

```
    ?      O      V
```

E.g. oppidum mūrum habet = the town has a wall

(N.B. oppidum could be nominative or accusative. But mūrum could only be accusative, because it goes like dominus. So if mūrum is the object, oppidum must be the subject.)

Study the information above about working with neuters. Then translate the following into English:

1 agricola scūtum portābat.

2 servus ad templum festīnābat.

3 nūntium dominī vocābās.

4 verba dominī timēbat.

5 prope mūrum dominī stābat.

6 incola scūta ad dominum portābat.

7 nautae bella nōn timēbant.

8 aquam et cibum ad oppidum portābāmus.

9 ad incolās scūta portābant.

10 dominus servōs dē bellō monet.

Exercise 4.17

Translate into Latin:

1 The master was building temples.

2 The woman does not have a shield.

3 'Master, we do not fear the dangers of war.'

4 We do not fear the words of the goddess.

5 The woman was hurrying towards the town.

6 The farmers were carrying the shields of the inhabitants.

7 We carried the shields from the town.

8 'Farmers, I do not like temples!'

9 The sailors attacked the town with spears.

10 The farmers and sailors fear the danger.

◯ Passages for translation

So you are now more than ready to face your first passage for translation. A passage is simply a collection of sentences joined up into a continuous story. There is nothing difficult about it, whether you are translating *into* Latin or *out of* Latin. All the same rules that you have learnt apply.

Exercise 4.18

Read the passage and answer the questions that follow:

The wrath of Achilles

incolae <u>Graeciae</u> cum incolīs <u>Troiae</u> pugnābant. <u>Troiam</u> nōn superābant. incolae
<u>Troiae</u> incolās <u>Graeciae</u> timēbant sed pugnābant. sagittīs et gladiīs cum incolīs <u>Graeciae</u>
pugnābant.

ancilla, Chrysēis, prope <u>Troiam</u> habitābat. Agamemnōn, dominus <u>Graecōrum</u>, ancillam
5 vidēbat et amābat. ancillam ad <u>castra</u>* portābat.

deus Apollō <u>īrātus</u> erat. Chrysēis erat <u>fāmula</u> deī. ūnus <u>Graecōrum</u>, Calchas, dē ancillā
dominum monēbat. Calchas, <u>vātēs</u> nōtus, dē ancillā Graecōs monēbat. 'deus Apollō
ancillam amat', <u>inquit</u> Calchas. etiam Achillēs dominum monēbat. tandem Agamemnōn
ancillam deō dăbat sed <u>īrātus</u> erat; amīcum <u>Achillem</u> <u>nōn iam</u> amābat.

10 Achilles ancillam habēbat. ancilla, Brisēis, in <u>castrīs</u> habitābat. Agamemnōn ancillam
amīcī vidēbat et amābat. ancillam amīcī ad <u>castra sua</u> portābat. Achillēs <u>īrātus</u> erat et in
bellō <u>nōn iam</u> pugnābat.

Agamemnōn in proeliō pugnābat sed perīcula bellī timēbat. oppidum oppugnābat sed
Troiānōs timēbat. oppidum nōn superābat. Achillēs in bellō <u>nōn iam</u> pugnābat.

15 tandem Agamemnōn nūntiōs ad <u>Achillem</u> festīnāre iubēbat. nūntiī <u>Achillem</u> laudābant.
Achillēs tamen nōn pugnābat.

* The word castra is always found in the plural, even though the English translation (camp) is singular.

Graecia, -ae = Greece	vātēs (nom. sing.) = a prophet
Troia, -ae = Troy	inquit = (he) said
Graecī = the Greeks	suus = his own
castra, -ōrum, n. pl. = a camp	nōn iam = no longer
īrātus = angry	Achillem = Achilles (accusative)
fāmula, -ae, f. = attendant	

1 Translate the passage into English, writing your translation *on alternate lines*.

2 In line 1, in which tense is pugnābant?

   Present   Imperfect

3 In line 2, in which case is incolās?

   Nominative   Accusative   Genitive   Ablative

4 sagittīs et gladiīs (line 2): in which case are these words?

   Vocative   Accusative   Dative   Ablative

5 sed (line 2). What sort of word is this?

noun   conjunction   adverb   preposition

6 prope (line 4). What sort of word is this?

noun   verb   adverb   preposition

7 monēbat (line 7). What sort of word is this?

noun   verb   adverb   preposition

8 Complete the table below. The first one has been done for you.

Latin word from passage	Meaning of Latin word	English word derived
pugnābant (line 1)	they fought	pugnacious
habitābat (line 10)		
laudābant (line 15)		

9 nūntiōs (line 15) means *the messengers*. How would you say *the messenger* in Latin, keeping the case the same?

10 iubēbat (line 15) means *He ordered*. How would you say in Latin *He orders*?

Go further

There are lots of words in Latin to describe speaking, saying or telling:

nārrō = I tell
vocō = I call
rogō = I ask
dīcō = I say
clāmō = I shout
moneō = I warn

However, when we see direct speech quoted, inside inverted commas, it is usually accompanied by the rather peculiar-looking verb inquit (= he says) or inquiunt (= they say), even when what the speaker is actually doing is shouting or asking or warning, rather than simply saying.

E.g. 'Who is the queen?' asked the farmer.

'quis est rēgīna?' inquit agricola.

Exercise 4.19

Copy and complete the table below, to show the connection between Latin and English words. The first one has been done for you.

	Latin word	Meaning of Latin word	English word derived
	amat	he loves	amorous
1	monent		
2	mūrus		
3	verbōrum		
4	vident		
5	movēmus		
6	dominōrum		
7	templa		
8	equus		
9	serve		
10	bellī		

Vocabulary 4

Latin	English
Nouns in -us	
amīcus, amīcī, m.	friend
cibus, cibī, m.	food
dominus, dominī, m.	lord, master
equus, equī, m.	horse
gladius, gladiī, m.	sword
mūrus, mūrī, m.	wall
nūntius, nūntiī, m.	messenger
servus, servī, m.	slave
Nouns in -um	
bellum, bellī, n.	war
oppidum, oppidī, n.	town
perīculum, perīculī, n.	danger
scūtum, scūtī, n.	shield
templum, templī, n.	temple
verbum, verbī, n.	word
Verbs	
habeō, -ēre	I have
moneō, -ēre	I warn, advise
moveō, -ēre	I move
rīdeō, -ēre	I hold
timeō, -ēre	I fear
videō, -ēre	I see

The Trojan War

This topic is part of the Non-Linguistic Studies section of the ISEB syllabus.

In this chapter we have read about the wrath of Achilles. The Romans were fascinated by the history and mythology of Ancient Greece, and particularly the stories of the Trojan War.

The Trojan War owes its origin to the Judgement of Paris. When King Peleus was married to the sea-nymph Thetis, all the gods and goddesses were invited to the wedding, all except one: Eris the goddess of Discord. Eris was furious at the insult, and rolled a golden apple into the wedding feast, on which she had written 'For the most beautiful'. The goddesses fought over the apple, and Zeus, the king of the gods, sent them down to the fields outside Troy for their beauty to be judged by Paris. Paris was living as a shepherd-boy but was really the son of King Priam, and was shortly after this reunited with his father and received into the city as a prince of Troy.

Paris decided that the most beautiful goddess was Aphrodite, the goddess of love, and in return she promised him the most beautiful woman in the world. This was Helen, the wife of King Menelaus of Sparta, and when Paris seized Helen and took her back to Troy, war was declared. All the Greek princes, including Achilles (the semi-divine son of Thetis) and Odysseus (hero of so many stories loved by the Greeks), vowed to recover the queen, and sailed with a huge fleet under the command of Menelaus's brother Agamemnon, King of Mycenae.

The Greeks besieged the city of Troy and for ten long years the war dragged on. In the tenth year of the war, Agamemnon insulted the god Apollo by seizing the daughter of one of his priests. When Achilles tried to warn Agamemnon about the consequences of this, Agamemnon seized a slave-girl belonging to Achilles, and Achilles's wrath (or anger) was such that he withdrew to his tent and refused to fight any longer for the Greeks. Without Achilles fighting for them, the Greeks began to suffer heavy losses and it looked as if the war would be lost.

Exercise 4.20

Find out what you can about the origins of the Trojan War.

(a) Tell the story of the Judgement of Paris in your own words.

(b) Explain why Helen is sometimes referred to as 'the face that launched a thousand ships'.

■ The Judgement of Paris depicted on an altar dedicated by Tiberius Claudius Faventinus.

5 Adjectives; more on the 2nd declension

Adjectives

An adjective is used to describe a noun and must 'agree' with the noun it describes in gender, case and number. For example, if the *noun* is feminine, genitive singular, the *adjective* must be feminine, genitive singular.

Adjectives therefore, like nouns, need to have cases. But the good news is that you already know all the endings you need. Bonus is a 1st/2nd declension adjective and as you can see, it takes its endings from the nouns of the 1st and 2nd declensions which you have already learnt:

bonus, bona, bonum = good			
	Masculine	Feminine	Neuter
Nom.	bon-us	bon-a	bon-um
Voc.	bon-e	bon-a	bon-um
Acc.	bon-um	bon-am	bon-um
Gen.	bon-ī	bon-ae	bon-ī
Dat.	bon-ō	bon-ae	bon-ō
Abl.	bon-ō	bon-ā	bon-ō
Nom.	bon-ī	bon-ae	bon-a
Voc.	bon-ī	bon-ae	bon-a
Acc.	bon-ōs	bon-ās	bon-a
Gen.	bon-ōrum	bon-ārum	bon-ōrum
Dat.	bon-īs	bon-īs	bon-īs
Abl.	bon-īs	bon-īs	bon-īs

Agreement of adjectives

An adjective must 'agree' with the noun it describes. This means it must be in the same case (nominative, vocative, accusative, etc.), the same gender (masculine, feminine or neuter) and the same number (singular or plural). Adjectives in Latin usually come after their nouns, so when translating into Latin, do the noun first; then work out which gender, case and number the noun is; then select that form of the adjective.

E.g. Of the master = dominī
Masculine, genitive singular
Of the **good** master = dominī **bonī**

E.g. For the sailor = nautae
Masculine, dative singular
For the **good** sailor = nautae **bonō**

Exercise 5.1

Study the information above about adjectives. Adjectives ending in -us go like bonus and are always listed with their masculine, feminine and neuter endings. E.g. multus, multa, multum (or multus, -a, -um) = much, many. Give the following:

1 Masc. acc. pl. of malus, -a, -um = bad

2 Fem. dat. sing. of fessus, -a, -um = tired

3 Neut. abl. pl. of īrātus, -a, -um = angry

4 Masc. nom. pl. of altus, -a, -um = high, deep

5 Fem. gen. sing. of magnus, -a, -um = big, great

Exercise 5.2

Translate the following into English:

1 ad puellās fessās

2 nautam bonum

3 prope agricolam īrātum

4 perīculum magnum

5 puellārum parvārum

6 servōrum fessōrum

7 bellī magnī

8 'domine īrāte'

9 cum dominīs Rōmānīs

10 scūta magna

Exercise 5.3

Give the Latin, using prepositions where necessary, for:

1 In great danger

2 Of the bad slave

3 'O good sailors!'

4 Out of the big island

5 For the tired farmer

6 In the great battle

7 With the good inhabitants

8 Through the deep water

9 Against the angry master

10 Of the small girls

Exercise 5.4

Study the following sentences. To ensure correct translation, we have put brackets around the nouns and adjectives that go together. Translate into English:

1 [dominus īrātus] [servum malum] vocābat.

2 [agricolae fessī] terram parābant.

3 [multī agricolae] incolam [hastīs longīs] superābant.

4 [dominī malī] [servōs fessōs] nōn amant.

5 incolās [hastīs magnīs] et [multīs sagittīs] superābant.

6 [agricola īrātus] [equum malum] vocat.

7 [incolae bonī] aquam dominō parābant.

8 [multa templa] prope oppidum aedificābant.

9 nūntiī [servōs malōs] vocant.

10 [multa scūta] et [hastās magnās] parābant.

Exercise 5.5

Translate into English:

1 amīcus bonus servum malum monēbat.

2 nautae fessī aquam altam timēbant.

3 multī incolae templum magnum aedificābant.

4 dominus malus scūtum magnum habēbat.

5 templum mūrīs magnīs aedificant.

6 dea īrāta oppidum tuum nōn amat.

7 amīcus tuus rēgīnam saevam nōn vidēbat.

8 multa perīcula bellī timēbāmus.

9 servī in templō magnō rīdēbant.

10 fēminae multa scūta et mūrum magnum vidēbant.

Exercise 5.6

Translate into Latin:

1 My daughter loves your friend.

2 Your friend loves the queen.

3 They have big walls.

4 I warn the tired slaves.

5 The messengers were warning the tired inhabitants.

6 She is singing in the big temple.

7 The words of the master were savage.

8 I do not like the new master.

9 He was giving food to the tired slave-girls.

10 We saw many horses in the street.

Puer and magister

You have met the two main types of 2nd declension noun: dominus and bellum. Now there are two more types to learn, both very similar.

	puer, pueri, m. = boy	magister, magistri, m. = master, teacher
Nom.	puer	magister
Voc.	puer	magister
Acc.	puer-um	magistr-um
Gen.	puer-ī	magistr-ī
Dat.	puer-ō	magistr-ō
Abl.	puer-ō	magistr-ō
Nom.	puer-ī	magistr-ī
Voc.	puer-ī	magistr-ī
Acc.	puer-ōs	magistr-ōs
Gen.	puer-ōrum	magistr-ōrum
Dat.	puer-īs	magistr-īs
Abl.	puer-īs	magistr-īs

These nouns use identical endings to dominus except in the nominative and vocative singular. The difference between the two is that nouns like puer 'keep their e' whereas nouns like magister 'drop their e'.

You have already learnt how to find a noun's stem by looking at its genitive singular. If the -er of the nominative has changed to -erī, then the noun goes like puer. But if the -er has changed to -rī (in other words if the 'e' has dropped out), it goes like magister.

E.g. ager, agrī, m. = 'field' goes like magister, because it has 'dropped its e'.

Note that the word magister refers to a master in the sense of school master, whereas dominus refers to a master in the sense of lord.

Exercise 5.7

Study the information above about nouns like puer and magister. Nouns like puer are quite rare (apart from puer itself), so if in doubt, 'drop the e'!

Write out in full:

1 liber, librī, m. = book

2 ager, agrī, m. = field

Exercise 5.8

Translate into English. As before, put brackets around the nouns and adjectives that go together before starting. Where there are prepositions, you may find you have to put a bracket around *three* words: the preposition, its noun and an adjective agreeing with the noun.

E.g. puella [ad agricolam bonum] ambulat = the girl walks towards the good farmer.

 1 [magister bonus] [puerum fessum] vocābat.

 2 puerōs [dē bellō magnō] rogābam.

 3 bella puer bonus nōn amat.

 4 in agrōs magnōs cum servīs festīnābat.

 5 magister īrātus puerum et servōs spectat.

 6 puerōs malōs nōn vocābam.

 7 agricola magnus in agrō labōrābat.

 8 puerum et servōs gladiō magnō superābat.

 9 puer et servī cum agricolā pugnābant.

10 magister puerō cibum nōn dăbat.

◯ Adjectives in -er

Just as some 2nd declension nouns end in -er rather than -us, so do some adjectives. And just as some nouns 'drop the e' and some don't, so it is with adjectives.

miser, misera, miserum = miserable, wretched		
	M	**F**	**N**
Nom.	miser	miser-a	miser-um
Voc.	miser	miser-a	miser-um
Acc.	miser-um	miser-am	miser-um
Gen.	miser-ī	miser-ae	miser-ī
Dat.	miser-ō	miser-ae	miser-ō
Abl.	miser-ō	miser-ā	miser-ō
Nom.	miser-ī	miser-ae	miser-a
Voc.	miser-ī	miser-ae	miser-a
Acc.	miser-ōs	miser-ās	miser-a
Gen.	miser-ōrum	miser-ārum	miser-ōrum
Dat.	miser-īs	miser-īs	miser-īs
Abl.	miser-īs	miser-īs	miser-īs

pulcher, pulchra, pulchrum = beautiful		
	M	**F**	**N**
Nom.	pulcher	pulchr-a	pulchr-um
Voc.	pulcher	pulchr-a	pulchr-um
Acc.	pulchr-um	pulchr-am	pulchr-um
Gen.	pulchr-ī	pulchr-ae	pulchr-ī
Dat.	pulchr-ō	pulchr-ae	pulchr-ō
Abl.	pulchr-ō	pulchr-ā	pulchr-ō
Nom.	pulchr-ī	pulchr-ae	pulchr-a
Voc.	pulchr-ī	pulchr-ae	pulchr-a
Acc.	pulchr-ōs	pulchr-ās	pulchr-a
Gen.	pulchr-ōrum	pulchr-ārum	pulchr-ōrum
Dat.	pulchr-īs	pulchr-īs	pulchr-īs
Abl.	pulchr-īs	pulchr-īs	pulchr-īs

You can tell whether an adjective in -er goes like miser or pulcher by studying its feminine and neuter forms, to see whether the 'e' has dropped or not.

E.g. noster, nostra, nostrum = 'our' goes like pulcher, because the 'e' has dropped out.

Exercise 5.9

Study the information above about adjectives in -er. Note how you can tell whether the adjective in -er goes like miser or pulcher by studying its feminine and neuter forms to see whether the 'e' has dropped out or not. Remember also that adjectives in -us go like bonus. Give the following forms:

1 Masc. gen. sing. of vester, vestra, vestrum = your (of you (plural))

2 Fem. dat. pl. of noster, nostra, nostrum = our

3 Neut. gen. pl. of miser, misera, miserum = wretched, miserable

4 Fem. abl. sing. of meus, mea, meum = my

5 Masc. acc. sing. of tuus, tua, tuum = your (of you (singular))

> Note how Latin has two words for 'your'. If you are talking to one person (i.e. you, singular), you use tuus. If you are talking to more than one person (i.e. you, plural), you use vester.
>
> E.g. 'Master, I love your daughter' = 'fīliam tuam, domine, amō.'
>
> E.g. 'Slaves, I love your master' = 'dominum vestrum, servī, amō.'

Exercise 5.10

Translate into English:

1 magistrī nostrī puellās fessās monēbant.

2 'librōs vestrōs, puerī malī, nōn laudō.'

3 puerī librōs ad oppidum rēgīnae portant.

4 librōs ad templum magnum nōn portābāmus.

5 magistrī librōs puellīs pulchrīs dăbant.

6 puellae pecūniam amābant sed magistrōs timēbant.

7 puer malus librum pulchrum in aquam altam portābat.

8 poēta clārus puellam pulchram spectābat.

9 puellās malās nōn amō.

10 puellae et puerī ē templō pulchrō ambulābant et in agrōs festīnābant.

Exercise 5.11

Translate into Latin:

1 The miserable farmer

2 My daughter

3 The beautiful temples

4 Of the beautiful girls

5 Our arrows

6 'O inhabitants, we looked at your beautiful land.'

7 We overcome many inhabitants with our swords.

8 'O Queen, we were calling your messengers.'

9 The tired sailors sail towards the beautiful island.

10 You do not overcome our country with arrows and spears.

Go further

Other modern languages

A very large number of words in English are derived from Latin, but the links are even stronger with other modern languages such as French, Spanish and Italian. This is because the Roman Empire covered much of Europe and beyond, and the Latin language that was spoken there for hundreds of years developed, gradually, into modern French, Italian, Spanish, etc. Notice how the spelling may change from language to language, but the Latin root is always clear. Notice, also, how English very often has a word which is clearly not derived from Latin (*carry* does not come from portō) and yet has associated words (*portable*) which clearly are:

Latin	English	French	Spanish	Italian
portāre	portable	porter	(trans)portar	portare

Exercise 5.12

Read the information above about other modern languages. Copy and complete the table of derivations below, using as many modern languages as you can.

Latin	English	French	Spanish	Italian
amāre				
dōnum				
amīcus				
bonus				
malus				
liber				

Exercise 5.13

Read the passage and answer the questions that follow:

The Trojan prince, Hector, kills Patroclus

Graecī diū Troiam oppugnābant nec tamen oppidum superābant. Achillēs in castrīs cum amīcō, Patroclō, manēbat. Graecī timēbant. Patroclus, amīcus bonus, in proelium festīnābat et cum Hectore pugnābat. Hector Patroclum superābat. Achillēs miser erat et in proelium festīnābat. Achillēs Patroclum ad castra sua portābat et flēbat.

> Graecī = the Greeks
> nec tamen = but ... not
> castra, -ōrum, n. pl. = camp
> Hectore (abl.) = Hector
> fleō, -ēre = I weep

1 diū (line 1). What part of speech is this?

   a noun   a verb   an adverb   a preposition

2 oppugnābant (line 1).

   (a) In which person is this verb?

      1st   2nd   3rd

   (b) What would it be if it were in the 3rd person singular?

      oppugnābam   oppugnābat   oppugnābās

3 amīcō (line 2).

   (a) In which case is this word?

      vocative   ablative   dative   genitive

   (b) What would it be if it were plural?

      amīcōrum   amīcīs   amīcōs

4 bonus (line 2).

   (a) What part of speech is this word?

      a pronoun   an adjective   a verb   a noun

   (b) With which word does it agree?

      amīcus   in   proelium

5 proelium (line 3). In which case is this word?

   nominative   vocative   accusative   genitive

6 Copy and complete the table below. The first one has been done for you.

Latin word from passage	Meaning of Latin word	English word which comes from the Latin word
amīcō (line 2)	friend	amicable
miser (line 3)		
portābat (line 4)		

7 portābat (line 4).

   (a) In which person is this verb?

        1st   2nd   3rd

   (b) Give the number of this verb

        singular   plural

   (c) Who is the subject of this verb?

        Achillēs   Patrōclum   castra

8 Complete the following Latin sentence:

   The friends call the master.

   amīcī _____ vocant.

   dominus   dominum   dominōs   dominī

9 Which of these Latin sentences means 'The slave-girl is calling the farmer'?

   ancilla agricolās vocat.   agricola ancillam vocat.

   ancillae agricolam vocat.   ancilla agricolam vocat.

10 Complete the following sentence:

   We overcome the inhabitants.

   incolās _____

   superat   superās   superātis   superāmus

Go further

The Latin for 'but … not' is nec tamen. The Romans would only very rarely have used sed nōn.

E.g. He loves war but does not fight = bellum amat nec tamen pugnat.

Similarly, the Latin for 'and … not' is nec. Again, the Romans would not have used 'et nōn'.

E.g. He fears war and does not fight = bellum timet **nec** pugnat.

Exercise 5.14

Translate into Latin:

1 We love our country.

2 You (pl.) love your daughter.

3 'Master, we do not like your books.'

4 'O masters, we do not like your books.'

5 They built a big wall near the water.

6 The Romans were overcoming the inhabitants of the country.

7 'O girls, you were warning your friend.'

8 'O Queen, the inhabitants of the country love your temples.'

9 We prepare the food in the field of the tired farmer.

10 You (sing.) were not warning your masters.

◯ Vocabulary 5

Latin	English
Adjectives in -us	
altus, -a, -um	high, deep
bonus, -a, -um	good
fessus, -a, -um	tired
magnus, -a, -um	big, great
malus, -a, -um	bad
multus, -a, -um	much, many
novus, -a, -um	new
parvus, -a, -um	small
Rōmānus, -a, -um	Roman
saevus, -a, -um	savage
tuus, -a, -um	your (of you (sing.))
Adjectives in -er	
miser, misera, miserum	miserable
noster, nostra, nostrum	our
pulcher, pulchra, pulchrum	beautiful
sacer, sacra, sacrum	sacred
vester, vestra, vestrum	your (of you (pl.))
Nouns in -er	
ager, agrī, m.	field
liber, librī, m.	book
magister, magistrī, m.	master
puer, puerī, m.	boy

The deaths of Patroclus and Hector

This topic is part of the Non-Linguistic Studies section of the ISEB syllabus.

In the last chapter we learnt about the origins of the Trojan War. We will now hear how it drew towards a close.

When Achilles withdrew from the fighting, the Trojans found that they were able to push the Greeks back towards their camp and began setting fire to their ships. All appeared to be lost. So Patroclus, Achilles's best friend, put on Achilles's armour and went back into the fighting. At first everyone fled from him, thinking that it was Achilles. But Hector, the son of the King of Troy, encountered him and after a brief fight, killed him with a spear.

Achilles was heartbroken when he heard about the death of his friend, and was persuaded to return to the fighting. Vowing revenge on Hector, he chased the prince around the walls of Troy and eventually cut him down and dragged his bloody corpse behind his chariot, back to the Greek camp.

Achilles then showed his cruel side. Every day he would go out in his chariot and drag the blood-caked body of Hector around Patroclus's tomb. He would then leave it out in the heat of the day to rot. Eventually, however, Hector's father, the aged king Priam, came to Achilles and pleaded with him to return the body. The body was returned and a long truce was arranged while funeral games took place for the dead prince. The war then resumed.

Exercise 5.15

Find out what you can about the Trojan War.

(a) Tell the story of either the death of Patroclus or the death of Hector.

(b) How did the death you have written about affect the course of the war?

■ Achilles drags the corpse of Hector behind his chariot —
from a mosaic in Rome

6 The 3rd and 4th conjugations; questions

So now to finish off the verbs. We have met amō and moneō, and learnt to tell them apart by studying their principal parts. Verbs in -ō, -āre go like amō; verbs in -eō, -ēre go like moneō. In this chapter we will meet two more conjugations, the 3rd and 4th.

Verbs like regō

Verbs of the 3rd conjugation go like regō. The endings for regō are similar to those which you have met before, but there are significant differences which should be noted carefully.

regō, regere = I rule			
Present Tense		**Imperfect Tense**	
reg-ō	I rule	reg-ēbam	I was ruling
reg-is	You rule	reg-ēbās	You were ruling
reg-it	He, she, it rules	reg-ēbat	He, she, it was ruling
reg-imus	We rule	reg-ēbāmus	We were ruling
reg-itis	You rule	reg-ēbātis	You were ruling
reg-unt	They rule	reg-ēbant	They were ruling

Problems with regō

1 The present stem of regō is found in the 2nd principal part by chopping off -ere (rather than just -re as is normal).
2 The 2nd principal part of regō ends in -ere, just like the 2nd principal part of moneō. The difference is that verbs like regō go -ō, -ere, whereas verbs like moneo go -eō, -ēre. The 'ē' of monēre is pronounced long (to rhyme with *hairy*), whereas in regere it is short (to rhyme with *Gregory*).

Exercise 6.1

Study the information above about verbs like regō. Write out the present tense of the following. They may not all go like regō.

1 bibō, bibere = I drink

2 surgō, surgere = I rise, get up

3 mittō, mittere = I send

4 terreō, terrēre = I terrify, frighten

Exercise 6.2

Write out in the imperfect tense:

1 currō, currere = I run

2 legō, legere = I read, choose

3 dūcō, dūcere = I lead

4 scrībō, scrībere = I write

Exercise 6.3

Translate into English:

1 bibunt.

2 discēdēbant.

3 mittitis.

4 currit.

5 dūcēbat.

6 scrībunt.

7 bibēbat.

8 legēbat.

9 regēbat.

10 legitis.

11 legēbant.

12 mittēbāmus.

13 currēbātis.

14 legis.

15 scribēbam.

16 discēdunt.

17 dīcunt.

18 currunt.

19 bibimus.

20 regēbant.

Exercise 6.4

Translate into Latin:

1 I was ruling.

2 They were running.

3 You (sing.) drink.

4 We write.

5 You (pl.) do not lead.

6 I was saying.

7 She leads.

8 They were leading.

9 I departed.

10 She was ruling.

11 You (pl.) were departing.

12 You (pl.) are departing.

13 They are reading.

14 You (sing.) choose.

15 She runs.

16 We were drinking.

17 You (sing.) do not drink.

18 They lead.

19 We were reading.

20 They send.

Exercise 6.5

Translate into English:

1 nauta bibit.

2 puer fessus discēdēbat.

3 dominus nūntiōs mittit.

4 puerī et puellae currunt.

5 Rōmānī equōs dūcēbant.

6 magister novus nōn scrībit.

7 amīcī nostrī aquam bibēbant.

8 puellae pulchrae librōs legēbant.

9 agricola ex agrō discēdēbat.

10 librum poētae Rōmānī legis.

Exercise 6.6

Translate into English:

1 agricolae in agrō bibēbant.

2 puerī ē templō discēdēbant.

3 rēgīna ancillās ad fēminam mittēbat.

4 puerī et puellae ad mūrum currēbant.

5 Rōmānī multōs servōs ad oppidum magnum dūcēbant.

6 dominum novum nōn timēmus.

7 servī nostrī aquam bibunt.

8 puellae parvae librum in templō legēbant.

9 agricola fīliam rēgīnae magnopere timēbat.

10 nūntiī poētam ad dominum numquam mittunt.

Exercise 6.7

Translate into Latin:

1 I was not ruling the slaves.

2 The girls were running.

3 The savage master was drinking.

4 They lead the horses into the field.

5 He was saying bad words.

6 The poet was writing a book.

7 We were reading the books.

8 They were sending messengers to the master.

9 She rules the great country.

10 You (pl.) fear many dangers.

Questions in Latin

A question may be either general ('Are you running?') or specific ('Why are you running?'). These two types of question are put into Latin as follows:

1 Putting -ne on the end of the first word in the sentence.
   E.g. Are you running? = currisne?
2 Using a questioning word, such as quis = who? quid = what? cūr = why? or ubi = where?
   E.g. Why are you running? = cūr curris?
   E.g. Who is singing? = quis cantat?
   E.g. What were you drinking? = quid bibēbās?

Exercise 6.8

Study the information above about questions in Latin. Then translate into English:

1 cūr in agrīs currēbant?

2 'bibitisne in agrīs, ō agricolae?'

3 quis in agrīs ambulābat?

4 ubi habitābātis?

5 quis puerōs saevōs timēbat?

6 ubi labōrābātis, agricolae?

7 quis incolās patriae magnae regit?

8 magisterne puerōs et puellās vidēbat?

9 cūr puerī et puellae magistrum novum amant?

10 incolāsne sagittīs et gladiīs superābātis?

Exercise 6.9

Translate into Latin:

1 Does the tired farmer drink the water?

2 Was the sailor leading the inhabitants to the island?

3 Does the master see the small boys?

4 Why is the master reading the book?

5 Were we overcoming the inhabitants in the war?

6 Why is the tired farmer standing in the field?

7 Where is the beautiful queen?

8 Are the slaves departing from the country?

9 Were you (sing.) leading your friends into the field?

10 Who is the well-known farmer's daughter?

Exercise 6.10

From which Latin words do the following English words derive? Translate the Latin words and explain the meaning of the English words. The first one has been done for you.

Nautical   nauta = sailor.   Nautical means 'to do with sailing'.

1 Miserable   5 Magnify   9 Scribe

2 Agriculture   6 Amicable   10 Legible

3 Multiply   7 Imbibe

4 Library   8 Dominate

◯ Verbs like audiō

Verbs of the 4th conjugation go like audiō. Audiō is very similar to regō, copying the spelling (although not the pronunciation) of its endings almost exactly. Verbs like audiō have principal parts which go -iō, -īre. The present stem is found in the second principal part by chopping off -re (audī-).

audiō, audīre = I hear			
Present Tense		**Imperfect Tense**	
audi-ō	I hear	audi-ēbam	I was hearing
audī-s	You hear	audi-ēbās	You were hearing
audi-t	He, she, it hears	audi-ēbat	He, she, it was hearing
audī-mus	We hear	audi-ēbāmus	We were hearing
audī-tis	You hear	audi-ēbātis	You were hearing
audi-unt	They hear	audi-ēbant	They were hearing

Points to note with audiō:

- The present tense endings are the same as for amō and moneō except in the 3rd person plural where it goes -unt like regō instead of -nt.

- The imperfect is identical to regō.

- Verbs like audiō have principal parts which begin -iō, -īre.

Exercise 6.11

Study the information above about verbs like audiō. Write out the following tenses of the following verbs:

1 Present tense of dormiō, dormīre = I sleep

2 Present tense of veniō, venīre = I come

3 Imperfect tense of dormiō, dormīre = I sleep

4 Imperfect tense of veniō, venīre = I come

Exercise 6.12

Translate into English:

1 audiēbat.

2 monetne?

3 dormiēbat.

4 veniēbat.

5 currēbat.

6 cūr dormiēbant?

7 dăbat.

8 dormit.

9 quis dūcēbat?

10 dormiēbātis.

Exercise 6.13

Translate into Latin:

1 He was sleeping.

2 We were coming.

3 They were listening.

4 You (pl.) are sleeping.

5 You (sing.) were sleeping.

6 They listen.

7 They listened.

8 She sleeps.

9 She was sleeping.

10 They come.

Exercise 6.14

Translate into English:

1 puella magistrum nōn audiēbat.

2 quis puellam dē perīculō monet?

3 puella nōn audiēbat sed dormiēbat.

4 magister ad puellam veniēbat.

5 puella ad magistrum currēbat.

6 cūr amīcī in agrō dormiēbant?

7 puella magistrō librum magnum dăbat.

8 magister miser nōn dormit.

9 puellane amīcōs in viam dūcēbat?

10 magister sub mūrō dormiēbat.

Adverbs

Adverbs are mainly used to describe *how* or *when* things are done, e.g. quickly, slowly, well, often, etc. In Latin they are easy, as they do not have endings to change like nouns or adjectives, and simply have to be learnt as pieces of vocabulary. You have already learnt the adverb nōn = not, and the words cūr? and ubi? are also adverbs. Others to learn are:

igitur = therefore
magnopere = greatly, very much
numquam = never
quod = because
quoque = also
subitō = suddenly
tamen = however

Exercise 6.15

Read the passage and answer the questions that follow:

The first Roman traitress

Rōmulus incolās regēbat; incolae Rōmānī contrā Sabīnōs in bellō pugnābant. Tarpeia puella Rōmāna erat. aquam in oppidum puella portābat. puella fessa erat. Tarpeia Sabīnōs vidēbat. Sabīnī puellam nōn vidēbant. Sabīnī puellam nōn audiēbant. Sabīnī scūta magna et armillās pulchrās habēbant. Tarpeia armillās amābat et clāmābat: 'armillās vestrās amō,'
5 inquit. 'armillās vestrās magnopere cupiō.' Tarpeia Sabīnōs in oppidum dūcēbat quod armillās magnopere cupiēbat. Sabīnī tamen puellam malam nōn amābant. in oppidum ambulābant et armillās puellae malae dăbant. sed scūta quoque puellae malae dăbant. scūta magna in* puellam miseram iaciēbant. scūtīs magnīs puellam scelestam superābant et necābant.

*Note how in + acc. can mean 'at' in the sense of throwing something 'at' someone.

Sabīnī, masc. pl. = the Sabines
armilla, -ae, f. = bracelet
inquit = she said
cupiō = I want
iaciō = I throw
scelestus, -a, -um = wicked

1 Romānī contrā Sabīnōs in bellō pugnābant (line 1). What were the Romans doing?

2 Tarpeia puella Rōmāna erat (lines 1–2). Who was Tarpeia?

3 aquam in oppidum puella portābat (line 2). What was Tarpeia doing?

4 Sabīnī scūta magna …Tarpeia armillās amābat (lines 3–4). What were the Sabines carrying and why was this of interest to Tarpeia?

5 clāmābat: 'armillās … cupiō.' (line 4). What did Tarpeia shout?

6 Tarpeia … magnopere cupiēbat (lines 5–6). Why did Tarpeia agree to lead the Sabines into the town?

7 incolās (line 1). In which case is this word?

Nominative   Accusative   Genitive   Ablative

8 pugnābant (line 1). In which tense is this verb?

Present   Imperfect

9 oppidum (line 2). Why is this word in the accusative case?

Subject of the verb   Object of the verb   It follows the preposition in

10 fessa (line 2). What sort of word is this?

Verb   Adjective   Pronoun   Adverb

11 vestrās (line 4). What sort of word is this?

Verb   Adjective   Pronoun   Adverb

12 scūtīs (line 8). This word means 'with the shields'. How would you say in Latin 'with the shield'?

scūtō   scūta   scūtae   scūtī

13 miseram (line 8). Translate this word and give an English word derived from it.

14 Sabīnī tamen … necābant (lines 8–9). Translate these lines into English.

Exercise 6.16

Copy and complete the table below. The first one has been done for you.

	Latin word	Meaning of Latin	English word derived
	dominōs	the masters	dominate
1	dūcēbant		
2	librōs		
3	audiēbāmus		
4	regunt		
5	novus		

	Latin word	Meaning of Latin	English word derived
6	trāns		
7	scrībunt		
8	magister		
9	dormiēbant		
10	amīcōs		

◯ Vocabulary 6

Latin	English
Verbs	
audiō, audīre	I hear
bibō, bibere	I drink
currō, currere	I run
dormiō, dormīre	I sleep
dīcō, dīcere	I say
discēdō, -ere	I depart
dūcō, dūcere	I lead
legō, legere	I read, choose
mittō, mittere	I send
regō, regere	I rule
scrībō, scrībere	I write
veniō, venīre	I come
Pronouns	
quid?	What?
quis?	Who?
Adverbs	
cūr?	Why?
-ne ...?	Asks a question
ubi?	Where?
igitur	therefore
magnopere	greatly
numquam	never

Horatius saves Rome

This topic is part of the Non-Linguistic Studies section of the ISEB syllabus.

From its foundation by Romulus, Rome was ruled by a succession of seven kings until 510 BC when the last of these, Tarquin the Proud, was driven out of the city by the people. Furious at this, he sought help from the neighbouring Etruscan king, Lars Porsenna, King of Clusium. Lars Porsenna marched on Rome at the head of a huge army of Etruscans. He captured the Janiculum hill and was preparing to cross the River Tiber at the Pons Sublicius. But it was here that a brave Roman called Horatius Cocles took up his station, determined to save the city. He realised that the only way to frustrate the enemy was to destroy the bridge before they could cross. So, calling for assistance from two companions, Spurius Lartius and Titus Herminius, Horatius held off the Etruscan army, while the rest of the Romans began to hack away at the bridge. As soon as the bridge was about to collapse, Horatius sent his two companions back to safety while he himself continued to hold off the enemy single-handed.

Suddenly, with an almighty crash, the Pons Sublicius fell into the Tiber. Horatius had saved Rome. Then, holding his arms up in prayer, the young man called upon the river god, Father Tiber, with the words 'accept this man and these arms into your waters'. He then leapt, fully armed, into the river and swam to safety on the other side.

Exercise 6.17

Find out what you can about Lars Porsenna and his war with Rome.

(a) Tell the story of how Horatius saved Rome.

(b) Which qualities in Horatius do you think the Romans particularly admired?

■ Horatius and his two companions at the Pons Sublicius – an artist's impression

The mixed conjugation; Roman numerals

Verbs like capiō

There is one more conjugation, called the *mixed conjugation*, which is a combination of the 3rd and 4th.

capiō, capere = I capture, I take			
Present Tense		**Imperfect Tense**	
capi-ō	I capture	capi-ēbam	I was capturing
cap-is	You capture	capi-ēbās	You were capturing
cap-it	He, she, it captures	capi-ēbat	He, she, it was capturing
cap-imus	We capture	capi-ēbāmus	We were capturing
cap-itis	You capture	capi-ēbātis	You were capturing
capi-unt	They capture	capi-ēbant	They were capturing

Mixed conjugation verbs go like capiō.

- Although they start -iō (like audiō), their 2nd principal part goes -ere (like regō).
- Their endings are exactly like audiō **when this leads to two vowels together** (e.g. capiō, capiunt, capiēbam, etc.), and like regō when this is not the case (e.g. capis, capit, capimus, etc.).
- For the time being (apart from the present infinitive in -ere) this only affects the pronunciation of the i in the present tense, so treat capiō like audiō and you will be fine.

Exercise 7.1

Study the information above about verbs like capiō. Note how they can be recognised by the fact that, although their 1st principal part goes -iō (like audiō), their 2nd principal part goes -ere (like regō). Write out the following:

1 Present tense of cupiō, cupere = I want, desire

2 Present tense of iaciō, iacere = I throw

3 Imperfect tense of faciō, facere = I do, make

Exercise 7.2

Translate into English:

1 cupimus.
2 facitis.
3 iacitis.
4 capiēbat.
5 faciēbant.

6 capiēbāmus.
7 cupiēbat.
8 cupitis.
9 iaciēbam.
10 capere.

Exercise 7.3

Translate into Latin:

1 He was capturing.
2 She was throwing.
3 They take.
4 You (pl.) want.
5 To throw.

6 They were taking.
7 He was throwing.
8 To do.
9 To make.
10 You (sing.) were taking.

Exercise 7.4

Translate into English:

1 quis cupit oppidum oppugnāre?
2 'quid facis, puer?'
3 'cūr aquam iacitis, ancillae?'
4 incolae in templō numquam dormiunt.
5 ubi est fīlia rēgīnae?
6 Rōmānī puellam malam capiēbant.
7 dominus servōs miserōs in agrum dūcere cupiēbat.
8 puerī et puellae librōs legere cupiunt.
9 servī malī cibum in aquam iaciēbant.
10 agricola equum fessum trāns aquam dūcere nōn cupiēbat.

Roman numerals

The numerals we use are Arabic numerals (1, 2, 3, etc.). The Romans, as you would expect, used Roman numerals (I, II, III, etc.). Numerals, when written as *words*, may be cardinal (one, two, three, etc.) or ordinal (first, second, third, etc.). The numerals from 1 to 10 are as follows:

Numerals	Cardinals	Ordinals
I	ūnus	prīmus
II	duǒ	secundus
III	trēs	tertius
IV/IIII	quattuor	quārtus
V	quīnque	quīntus
VI	sex	sextus
VII	septem	septimus
VIII	octo*	octāvus
IX	novem	nōnus
X	decem	decimus

*The final o of octo can be pronounced long or short.

Of the numerals, only ūnus, duǒ and trēs decline (you will learn how later). Ordinals decline like bonus and must agree with the noun they describe.

E.g. the first boy = puer prīmus; the first girl = puella prīma; etc.

Note that the Roman year began in March and originally contained only ten months. This explains why the months September–December are derived from the Latin for 7–10 (and not 9–12 as one would expect).

Exercise 7.5

Translate into English:

1 ūnus agricola; agricola prīmus

2 duǒ dominī; dominus secundus

3 trēs nūntiī; nūntius tertius

4 quattuor sagittae; sagitta quārta

5 quīnque oppida; oppidum quīntum

6 sex equī; equus sextus

7 septem poētae; poēta septimus

8 octo īnsulae; īnsula octāva

9 novem rēgīnae; rēgīna nōna

10 decem mūrī; mūrus decimus

Exercise 7.6

Study the information above about Roman numerals. Then give the Latin for:

1 One boy; the first boy

2 Two farmers; the second farmer

3 Three sailors; the third sailor

4 Four girls; the fourth girl

5 Five women; the fifth woman

6 Six masters; the sixth master

7 Seven Romans; the seventh Roman

8 Eight arrows; the eighth arrow

9 Nine shields: the ninth shield

10 Ten islands; the tenth island

Exercise 7.7

From which Latin words do the following derive? Give and translate the Latin word and explain the meaning of the English one, showing the connection between the English and Latin. The first one has been done for you.

Insulate   īnsula = island. To insulate is to surround (as water surrounds an island).

1 Octet

2 Quintuplets

3 Duet

4 Prime

5 Tertiary

6 Quartet

7 Secondary

8 October

9 November

10 December

Exercise 7.8

Translate into English:

1 ūnus equus in agrō stābat.

2 trēs ancillae prope templum dormiēbant.

3 quīnque amīcōs magnopere amat.

4 septem servōs et decem ancillās habēbat rēgīna nostra.

5 ubi sunt novem gladiī?

6 Rōmānī quattuor servōs ex oppidō dūcēbant.

7 Mārcus erat dominus tertius meus.

8 quis erat secunda rēgīna oppidī parvī?

9 magister librum prīmum legere cupit.

10 decem agricolās laudābāmus.

◯ fīlius, deus, vir

The following nouns are 2nd declension but have some slightly strange forms. Strange forms are shown in bold.

Nom.	fīlius = son	deus = god	vir = man
Voc.	**fīlī**	**deus**	**vir**
Acc.	fīlium	deum	virum
Gen.	fīliī (or **fīlī**)	deī	virī
Dat.	fīliō	deō	virō
Abl.	fīliō	deō	virō
Nom.	fīliī	**dī** (or deī)	virī
Voc.	fīliī	**dī** (or deī)	virī
Acc.	fīliōs	deōs	virōs
Gen.	fīliōrum	deōrum (or **deum**)	virōrum (or **virum**)
Dat.	fīliīs	**dīs** (or deīs)	virīs
Abl.	fīliīs	**dīs** (or deīs)	virīs

Go further

Both fīlius and deus have 1st declension feminine versions (fīlia = daughter and dea = goddess), which you have already met. These decline like puella but, to avoid confusion in the dative and ablative plural, they go fīliābus and deābus.

Exercise 7.9

Translate into English:

1 fīlius parvus magistrī ad oppidum novum festīnābat.

2 agricolae trēs equōs ad fīliam rēgīnae dūcēbant.

3 septem puellae dīs prope mūrōs oppidī cantābant.

4 sex puerī per viās oppidī novī currēbant.

5 tandem ex oppidō veniēbat et in agrōs festīnābat.

6 sex virī et septem fēminae cum dominō discēdēbant.

7 ad oppidum novum Rōmānī numquam veniēbant.

8 multī incolae equum pulchrum habēre cupiēbant.

9 dī templum sacrum Rōmānōrum nōn amābant.

10 cūr verba virī saevī timētis?

Go further

In Latin, a vowel is always long when followed by ns or nf. Note that this even applies to the word in when it comes before a word beginning with s or f.

E.g. īn suō agrō = in his field.

Exercise 7.10

Study the information above about fīlius, deus and vir. Note the strange forms for fīlia and dea in the dative and ablative plural. Then translate into Latin, taking particular care with nos. 9 and 10:

1 We saw the men.

2 They feared the savage gods.

3 I hear the sons of the master.

4 The son of a god ruled the Romans.

5 The Romans were singing to the gods.

6 The men gave gifts to the goddess.

7 The good man was giving a horse to the daughter of the queen.

8 The gods warned the wretched men about the war.

9 I was giving a gift to my sons and daughters.

10 We gave gifts to the gods and goddesses.

Exercise 7.11

Read the passage and answer the questions that follow:

Ulysses and the trick of the wooden horse

Graecī oppidum Troiam diū oppugnābant nec tamen superābant. bellum longum erat. ūnus
Graecōrum, Ulixēs, callidissimus erat. ad patriam suam revenīre magnopere cupiēbat.
fēminam suam et fīlium vidēre magnopere cupiēbat. equum ligneum aedificābat et prope
castra equum relinquēbat. in equō multōs virōs, multōs gladiōs, multās sagittās pōnēbat.
5 deinde Graecī ā Troiā nāvigābant.
   Troiānī laetī erant quod bellum nōn amābant. equum ligneum vidēbant et in oppidum portāre
cupiēbant. ūnus Troiānōrum, Lāocoōn, equum timēbat. 'Graecōs timeō' inquit. 'etiam dōna
Graecōrum timeō.' Troiānī tamen equum nōn timēbant et in oppidum portābant.
   tandem Troiānī in oppidō dormiēbant. Ulixēs et virī ex equō veniēbant et per viās oppidī
10 festīnābant. incolās gladiīs et hastīs necābant et oppidum incendēbant.

Graecī = the Greeks	ligneus, -a, -um = wooden
Troia = Troy	castra (acc.) = the camp
nec tamen = but ... not	relinquō = I leave
Ulixēs = Ulysses	Troiānī, -ōrum, m. pl. = the Trojans
callidissimus = very cunning	inquit = he said
reveniō, -īre = to come back, return	dōnum, -i, n. = gift
fēmina (here) = wife	incendō = I set fire to

1 Graecī oppidum Troiam diū oppugnābant (line 1).
   What were the Greeks doing for a long time?

2 bellum longum erat (line 1). How is the war described?

3 ūnus Graecōrum, Ulixēs, callidissimus erat (lines 1–2).
   Who was Ulysses and how is he described?

4 ad patriam ... vidēre magnopere cupiēbat (line 2).
   What did Ulysses want to do?

5 equum ligneum aedificābat ... sagittās pōnēbat (lines 3–4).
   Describe what Ulysses did to trick the Trojans.

6 bellum (line 1). In which case is this word?

   Nominative   Vocative   Accusative   Genitive

7 portāre (line 6).

   (a) What part of the verb is this?

       3rd singular present tense   2nd plural present tense

       Present infinitive   Present stem

   (b) What does it mean?

       He carries   They carry   We carry   To carry

■ The wooden horse of Troy – a modern replica in Turkey

8 oppidum (line 8).

    (a) In which case is this word?

        Nominative   Vocative   Accusative   Genitive

    (b) Why is this case used?

        It is the subject   It is the object
        It follows the preposition in   It follows portāre

9 Translate the passage into English.

◯ Vocabulary 7

Latin	English
Nouns	
deus, deī, m.	god
fīlius, fīliī, m.	son
vir, virī, m.	man
Numerals	
ūnus	one
duŏ	two
trēs	three
quattuor	four
quīnque	five
sex	six
septem	seven
octo	eight
novem	nine
decem	ten
prīmus, -a, -um	first
secundus, -a, -um	second
tertius, -a, -um	third
Verbs	
capiō, -ere	I capture, take
cupiō, -ere	I want, desire
faciō, -ere	I do, make
iaciō, -ere	I throw

◯ Mucius Scaevola

After Horatius had frustrated the efforts of Lars Porsenna by having the bridge destroyed (see Chapter 6), Lars Porsenna besieged Rome. After a while food began to run out in the city. Keen to help save his

> This topic is part of the Non-Linguistic Studies section of the ISEB syllabus.

fellow citizens from starvation, a young Roman patrician, Gaius Mucius, approached the enemy camp. Sneaking past the guards he made for the king's tent, resolved to kill Lars Porsenna and put an end to the war. However, Gaius Mucius mistook the king's paymaster for the king, and having killed him, was promptly arrested and dragged before Lars Porsenna.

When questioned as to his identity and his intentions, Gaius said that he was a Roman who had come to kill the king. 'I am a Roman citizen,' he said, 'and Roman citizens do not fear death. Nor am I alone in wanting to kill you. There are many more Roman citizens prepared to risk their lives to kill you. You will have to fight each one in turn.'

Lars Porsenna flew into a rage and threatened to have the young man burnt alive. But Gaius was not afraid. He thrust his right hand into the flames of a nearby brazier with the words 'I do not fear pain.' Lars Porsenna was impressed by this display of bravery and sent him back to Rome. Furthermore, he soon made peace with the Romans, perhaps because he was concerned that he would be unable to defeat a city of citizens such as Gaius Mucius.

As for Gaius Mucius, shortly after this he was rewarded with a piece of land, and was ever after nicknamed Scaevola ('left-handed'), on account of the fact that he was unable to use his heavily disfigured right hand.

Exercise 7.12

1 (a) Tell the story of Mucius Scaevola.

(b) What qualities in Gaius Mucius do you think Lars Porsenna admired?

2 (a) How did Odysseus use the trick of the wooden horse to overthrow the city of Troy?

(b) In what ways did Odysseus deserve his reputation as a master of trickery?

■ Mucius Scaevola deliberately burning his hand – from a stone relief

8 The perfect tense; principal parts

The perfect tense

The perfect tense is used to describe a *completed* action in the past (unlike the imperfect tense, which refers to *uncompleted* actions).

E.g. I have read the book (perfect tense)

E.g. I was reading the book (imperfect tense)

The perfect tense is formed by adding a set of endings to the **perfect stem**. Each verb has a perfect stem which is different, sometimes very different, from the present stem. The perfect tense endings are the same for all verbs of all conjugations.

amāv-ī	I have loved
amāv-istī	You (sing.) have loved
amāv-it	He, she, it has loved
amāv-imus	We have loved
amāv-istis	You (pl.) have loved
amāv-ērunt	They have loved

Principal parts

To understand how to form the perfect tense of all the other verbs, we need to explain how principal parts work. All Latin verbs have things called **principal parts**. These are the four main parts of the verb, from which all other parts can be formed. The principal parts of amō are as follows:

1	**2**	**3**	**4**
am-ō	amā-re	amāv-ī	amāt-um
I love	To love	I have loved	(supine)

- The *first principal part* is the 1st person singular of the present tense and gives us the basic meaning of the verb.
- The *second principal part* is the **present infinitive**, and is used to find the **present stem** of the verb (by chopping off the -re).

- The *third principal part* is the 1st person singular of the perfect tense, and is used to find the **perfect stem** of the verb (by chopping off the -ī).
- The *fourth principal part* is the supine. This is a very rare part of the verb, but is useful as it gives us (by chopping off the -um) the **supine stem**, used for forming some of the passive tenses of the verb (described later in the course).

Although you won't need that fourth principal part for a while, it is much easier to learn all four of a verb's principal parts now, rather than finding that you need to come back and learn it later.

Almost all 1st conjugation verbs form their principal parts in exactly the same way as amō does (i.e. -ō, -āre, -āvī, -ātum). Thus nāvigō = I sail has the following principal parts:

nāvig**ō**	nāvig**āre**	nāvig**āvī**	nāvig**ātum**
I sail	To sail	I have sailed	(supine)

Exercise 8.1

Read the information above about principal parts. Write out the principal parts and meaning of the following 1st conjugation verbs:

1 nāvigō
2 ambulō
3 vocō
4 labōrō
5 festīnō

6 habitō
7 oppugnō
8 portō
9 laudō
10 rogō

Exercise 8.2

Using the principal parts of the verbs from Exercise 8.1, write out the perfect tense of the following verbs:

1 nāvigō
2 ambulō
3 vocō
4 labōrō
5 festīnō

Principal parts to watch out for

Two 1st conjugation verbs have rather unusual principal parts. Once you have learnt them, however, their perfect tenses form as you would expect. Simply chop off the -ī and add the endings:

dō	dăre	dedī	dătum	I give
stō	stāre	stetī	stătum	I stand

ded-ī	stet-ī
ded-istī	stet-istī
ded-it	stet-it
ded-imus	stet-imus
ded-istis	stet-istis
ded-ērunt	stet-ērunt

Exercise 8.3

Translate into English:

1 nāvigāvimus.
2 amāre.
3 vocāvit.
4 labōrāvērunt.
5 festīnāvistis.
6 habitāvērunt.
7 oppugnāvī.

8 nōn portāvī.
9 nōn laudāvistī.
10 rogāre.
11 dedit.
12 habitāvistis.
13 intrāvimus.
14 stetērunt.

15 oppugnāvimus.
16 portāvistī.
17 rogāvimus.
18 aedificāvērunt.
19 ambulāvistī.
20 cantāvērunt.

Exercise 8.4

Read the information above about principal parts and the perfect tense. Then translate into Latin:

1 I have sailed.
2 You (sing.) have called.
3 You (sing.) have built.
4 They have worked.
5 She has hurried.
6 To attack
7 We have not asked.

8 He has killed.
9 You (pl.) have carried.
10 To praise
11 He has given.
12 They have attacked.
13 You (pl.) have stood.
14 We have entered.

15 You (sing.) have lived
16 I have praised.
17 She has killed.
18 They have carried.
19 We have given.
20 I have stood.

Exercise 8.5

You have now learnt three tenses plus the present infinitive of 1st conjugation verbs like amō. Taking care over which endings are being used, translate the following into English:

1 laudāmus.

2 portāre.

3 vocābat.

4 necāvērunt.

5 intrāvistis.

6 habitābant.

7 oppugnāre.

8 nōn superābam.

9 stant.

10 rogāvit.

11 ambulātis.

12 amābāmus.

13 cantāre.

14 festīnāvērunt.

15 labōrāvimus.

16 nāvigāvistī.

17 parāvit.

18 pugnābāmus.

19 spectāvistis.

20 vocāre.

Exercise 8.6

Translate into Latin:

1 We build.

2 To work.

3 You (sing.) have hurried.

4 We were sailing.

5 They were calling.

6 You (pl.) like.

7 To fight.

8 You (sing.) have entered.

9 I was not asking.

10 She does not work.

11 He has given.

12 I have attacked.

13 She was living.

14 You (pl.) enter.

15 We were praising.

16 She has killed.

17 To carry.

18 They have not asked.

19 He has stood.

20 They have not stood.

More on principal parts: the other conjugations

We have seen how the principal parts of amō work, and how they are used to help us form the perfect tense. We have seen how most 1st conjugation verbs have principal parts that go –ō, -āre, -āvī, -ātum.

We now need to learn the principal parts of verbs of the other regular conjugations.

2nd	moneō	monēre	monuī	monitum
3rd	regō	regere	rēxī	rēctum
4th	audiō	audīre	audīvī	audītum
Mixed	capiō	capere	cēpī	captum

With these conjugations, unlike the 1st conjugation, there is no pattern that the verbs regularly follow in the 3rd and 4th principal parts. You simply have to learn a verb's principal parts when you meet the verb, because unless you do, you will not know how the verb forms its perfect tense.

The good news, however, is that if you do know a verb's principal parts, you will be able to form its perfect tense without any difficulty. Simply go to the 3rd principal part, chop off the −ī (to get the perfect stem) and add the perfect tense endings.

2nd conjugation

Exercise 8.7

Some verbs (such as timeō) do not have a supine.

Copy out and learn the principal parts of the following 2nd conjugation verbs:

dēleō	dēlēre	dēlēvī	dēlētum	I destroy
habeō	habēre	habuī	habitum	I have
iubeō	iubēre	iussī	iussum	I order
maneō	manēre	mānsī	mānsum	I remain
moveō	movēre	mōvī	mōtum	I move
respondeō	respondēre	respondī	respōnsum	I answer
rīdeō	rīdēre	rīsī	rīsum	I laugh
teneō	tenēre	tenuī	tentum	I hold
terreō	terrēre	terruī	territum	I frighten
timeō	timēre	timuī	—	I fear
videō	vidēre	vīdī	vīsum	I see

1 Write out the perfect tense of the first three of these verbs.

2 Give the Latin for:

    (a) He has feared.

    (b) She has seen.

    (c) They have destroyed.

    (d) We have ordered.

    (e) You (pl.) have remained.

    (f) To answer.

    (g) They hold.

    (h) He has held.

3 Translate into English:

    (a) rīsit.

    (b) vīdit.

    (c) dēlēvērunt.

    (d) mānsimus.

    (e) respondistī.

    (f) tenēre.

    (g) monētis.

    (h) manēre.

Exercise 8.8

Translate the following into English:

1 habēmus.	6 vidēbant.	11 tenētis.	16 timuistī.
2 monēre.	7 dēlēre.	12 terrēbāmus.	17 vīdit.
3 movēbat.	8 nōn iubēbam.	13 habēre.	18 videt.
4 rīsērunt.	9 manent.	14 monuērunt.	19 dēlēvistis.
5 timuistis.	10 respondit.	15 rīdēmus.	20 tenēre.

Exercise 8.9

Translate into Latin:

1 You (pl.) have.

2 To warn.

3 You (sing.) have moved.

4 We were laughing.

5 They were fearing.

6 You (pl.) see.

7 To destroy.

8 You (sing.) have ordered.

9 I was not remaining.

10 She does not hold.

11 He has terrified.

12 I have advised.

13 She was moving.

14 You (pl.) warn.

15 We were moving.

16 She has laughed.

17 To fear.

18 They have not seen.

19 He has feared.

20 They have not remained.

3rd conjugation

Copy out and learn the principal parts of the following 3rd conjugation verbs.

bibō	bibere	bibī	-	I drink
cōnstituō	cōnstituere	cōnstituī	cōnstitūtum	I decide
cōnsūmō	cōnsūmere	cōnsūmpsī	cōnsūmptum	I eat
currō	currere	cucurrī	cursum	I run
dīcō	dīcere	dīxī	dictum	I say
discēdō	discēdere	discessī	discessum	I depart
dūcō	dūcere	dūxī	ductum	I lead
legō	legere	lēgī	lēctum	I read
lūdō	lūdere	lūsī	lūsum	I play
mittō	mittere	mīsī	missum	I send
ostendō	ostendere	ostendī	ostentum	I show
pōnō	pōnere	posuī	positum	I place
scrībō	scrībere	scrīpsī	scrīptum	I write

1 Write out the perfect tense of the first three of these verbs.

2 Give the Latin for:

    (a) She has run.   **(e)** You (sing.) have read.

    (b) He has said.   **(f)** I have shown.

    (c) We have departed.   **(g)** They have written.

    (d) They have led.   **(h)** To send.

3 Translate into English:

    (a) dīxit.   **(d)** scrīpsimus.   **(g)** bibitis.

    (b) dūxistis.   **(e)** lūsistī.   **(h)** ostendere.

    (c) posuērunt.   **(f)** cucurrit.

Translate the following into English:

1 bibimus.   4 discessērunt.   7 lēgit

2 currere.   5 dūxistis.   8 nōn mittēbat.

3 dīcēbat.   6 legit.   9 mittit.

10 mīsit.　　14 cōnsūmpsērunt.　　18 lūsit.

11 regitis.　　15 cōnstituimus.　　19 ostenditis.

12 rēxistis.　　16 cōnstituistī.　　20 ostendistis.

13 scrībere.　　17 lūdit.

Exercise 8.12

Translate into Latin:

1　I drink.

2　To say.

3　You (sing.) have run.

4　We were departing.

5　They were leading.

6　You (pl.) send.

7　To rule.

8　You (sing.) have written.

9　I am not deciding.

10　She does not eat.

11　He has played.

12　I have shown.

13　She was placing.

14　You (pl.) place.

15　We were drinking.

16　She has run.

17　To decide.

18　They have not departed.

19　He has led.*

20　They have not read.

*N.B. Many people misspell the past tense of the English verb 'to lead'. The past tense of 'he leads' is 'he led'.

4th and mixed conjugations

Exercise 8.13

Copy out and learn the principal parts of the following 4th and mixed conjugation verbs.

audiō	audīre	audīvī	audītum	I hear
dormiō	dormīre	dormīvī	dormītum	I sleep
veniō	venīre	vēnī	ventum	I come
capiō	capere	cēpī	captum	I capture, take
cupiō	cupere	cupīvī	cupītum	I want, desire
iaciō	iacere	iēcī	iactum	I throw

1　Write out the perfect tense of dormiō, veniō and iaciō.

2　Give the Latin for:

　(a)　She has slept.　　(b)　He has captured.　　(c)　We have thrown.

3 Translate into English:

(a) dormīvit.

(e) iacimus.

(b) cupīvērunt.

(f) vēnit.

(c) iēcistis.

(g) venit.

(d) capere.

(h) iacere.

Exercise 8.14

Read the passage and answer the questions that follow:

Tarquin the Proud seizes the throne

Servius Tullius Rōmam regēbat. Rōmānī, quod servus erat, dominum nōn amābant. Tullia, fīlia dominī, Rōmam regere cupiēbat. Lūciō Tarquiniō, virō magnō sed saevō, <u>nūpsit</u>. Lūcius Tarquinius Rōmam regere magnopere cupīvit. Tarquinius et Tullia <u>scelestī</u> erant. Tarquinius et Tullia ad <u>cūriam</u> vēnērunt et multa verba mala dē Serviō Tulliō
5 dīcēbant. Tarquinius in sellā dominī sēdit et rīsit. <u>populus</u> Rōmānus Tarquinium et Tulliam magnopere timēbat.

Servius Tullius in cūriam ambulāvit. Tarquinium vīdit et īrātus erat.

'cūr in <u>sellā</u> meā <u>sedēs</u>?' <u>inquit</u>. Tarquinius rīdēbat et Tullium ē cūriā <u>trāxit</u>. dominum ē curiā trāxit et in viam iēcit. ibi, gladiīs et hastīs, virum miserum servī Tarquiniī necāvērunt. <u>posteā</u>
10 Tarquinius dominus Rōmae erat et Rōmānōs regēbat.

nūbō, -ere, nūpsī + dat. = I am married to	sedeō, -ēre, sēdī = I sit
scelestus, -a, -um = wicked	inquit = he said
cūria, -ae, f. = Senate house	trahō, -ere, trāxī, tractum = I drag
populus, -ī, m. = the people	posteā = afterwards
sella, -ae, f. = chair	

1 Servius Tullius Rōmam regēbat (line 1). What do we learn about Servius Tullius?

2 Rōmānī ... nōn amābant (line 1). Why did the Romans not like him?

3 Tullia ... cupiēbat (line 2). What are we told about Servius Tullius's daughter?

4 Lūciō Tarquiniō ... scelestī erant (lines 2–4). How is Tullia's husband described? Make two points.

5 verba (line 4); in which case is this word?

Nominative   Ablative   Genitive   Accusative

6 dominī (line 5); in which case is this word?

Nominative   Ablative   Genitive   Accusative

7 vīdit (line 7).

   (a) In which tense is this verb?

     Present   Imperfect   Perfect

   (b) What would it become if we had wished to write 'they were seeing'?

     vident   vīdērunt   vidēbant   vidēbunt

8 Which of the following from the passage is a verb in the perfect tense?

   cupīvit (line 3)   erant (line 4)   dīcēbant (line 5)   sedēs (line 8)

9 Which of the following from the passage is a verb in the present infinitive?

   magnopere (line 6)   regere (line 2)   erat (line 1)   sedēs (line 8)

10 Translate the passage into English, writing your translation on alternate lines.

Go further

Apposition

When we say something like 'I was leading Julia, my friend, into the street' we are using apposition. The words 'my friend' are *in apposition* to 'Julia', because they *explain or describe* her and **must go in the same case** as she does.

E.g.   Iūliam, amīcam meam, in viam dūcēbam = I was leading Julia, my friend, into the street.

      Mārcus, amīcus meus, in viam festīnāvit = Marcus, my friend, has hurried into the street.

      amīcus Mārcī, puerī bonī, in viam festīnāvit = The friend of Marcus, a good boy, has hurried into the street.

Exercise 8.15

Study the information above about apposition. Then translate into English:

1 Tarquinius Superbus, dominus malus, Rōmānōs diū terrēbat.

2 Lucrētia, puella Rōmāna, fīlium Tarquiniī magnopere timēbat.

3 Rōmānī cum Tarquiniō, dominō saevō, pugnābant.

4 poēta dominō, virō magnō, cantābat.

5 Cassia, ancilla pulchra, aquam prope mūrum parvum posuit.

6 multōs equōs Mārcō, magistrō vestrō, dedimus.

7 tandem Rōmānī oppidum magnum dēlēvērunt.

8 'quis Lucrētiam, puellam Rōmānam, terruit?'

9 'quid facitis, puerī? quis cibum cōnsūmpsit?'

10 magister saevus puerīs miserīs clāmāvit.

Dealing with the simple past

We have seen that the imperfect tense (e.g. amābat) means 'he was loving' and that the perfect tense (e.g. amāvit) means 'he has loved'. But sometimes we may wish to use the simple past, e.g. *he loved*, or *he warned*, or *he walked*? Or *he did not love, did not warn* or *did not walk*. Which tense do we use for this?

1   If we wish to refer to an action, completed at some definite point of time in the past, we are using the *simple past*. This tense, which in Greek was distinct and called the *aorist*, did not have its own set of endings in Latin, but had to share the perfect tense endings.

    E.g. The girl *carried* the gift to the farmer = puella dōnum ad agricolam portāvit.

2   However, if we are referring to a continuous or incomplete action in the past, we use the imperfect tense.

    E.g. The girl *worked* on the island = puella in īnsulā labōrābat.

The result of all this is that the meanings of the imperfect and perfect tenses should be thought of as follows:

Imperfect: amābam = I was loving, I used to love OR I loved (continously over a period of time).

Perfect: amāvī = I have loved OR I loved.

Exercise 8.16

Read the passage and answer the questions that follow:

Ulysses in the land of the Lotus-eaters

post bellum longum et saevum, Graecī <u>domum</u> <u>revenīre</u> magnopere cupiēbant. fīliōs et fīliās, etiam <u>fēminās</u> et amīcōs vidēre cupiēbant. itaque ā terrā Troiānōrum Graecī discessērunt et ad patriam nāvigāvērunt.
  ventus tamen <u>nāvēs</u> nautārum miserōrum ad Āfricam <u>pellēbat</u>. locus pulcher erat <u>nec</u> Graecī
5 timēbant. hīc dominus Graecus, Ulixēs, aquam et cibum colligere cupiēbat. <u>dum</u> tamen aquam et cibum nautae <u>quaerunt</u>,* turbam incolārum vīdērunt. incolae <u>benignī</u> erant et cibum nautīs fessīs dedērunt.
  nautae cibum cōnsūmpsērunt et dormiēbant. in cibō, tamen, erat <u>frūctus lōtī</u>. Graecī <u>lōtum</u> cōnsūmpsērunt <u>nec iam</u> ad patriam suam nāvigāre cupiēbant. in terrā pulchrā manēre
10 cupiēbant.

Ulixēs nautās in <u>nāvēs</u> festīnāre iussit. 'cūr in terrā <u>barbarā</u> manētis?' inquit. 'cūr ad fēminās et amīcōs, etiam fīliōs et fīliās, nōn nāvigātis?' nautae tamen, <u>quasi ēbriī</u>, dormiēbant. Ulixēs tandem nautās ad <u>nāvēs trāxit</u> et ā terrā <u>barbarā</u> cum sociīs discessit.
* See Go further, below.

domum = (to) home	quaerō, -ere = I look for
reveniō = I return	benignus, -a, -um = kind
fēmina (here) = wife	frūctus lōtī = the lotus fruit
nāvēs (acc. pl.) = ships	nec iam = and no longer
pellō, -ere = I drive	barbarus, -a, -um = foreign
nec = and ... not	quasi = as if
colligō, -ere = I collect	ēbrius, -a, -um = drunk
dum = while	trahō, -ere, trāxī = I drag

1 post bellum ... cupiēbant (line 1). What did the Greeks wish to do after the war?

2 ā terrā ... nāvigāvērunt (lines 2–3). How were they intending to travel?

3 ventus tamen ... pellēbat (line 4). What was it that changed their plans?

4 hīc dominus ... colligere cupiēbat (line 5). What did Ulysses want to do when he reached land?

5 dum tamen ... benignī erant (lines 5–6). Whom did the Greek sailors see and how are they described?

6 Graecī lōtum ... manēre cupiēbant (lines 8–9). Explain the effect that the lotus plant had on the Greeks that ate it.

7 iussit (line11).

   (a) Which part of the verb is this?

      3rd sing. perfect   Present infinitive   3rd sing. present   2nd plural perfect

   (b) What would it become if the subject of this verb were plural?

      iussitis   iussērunt   iussistis   iussunt

8 From the first paragraph of the passage (lines 1–3), give and translate:

   (a) two examples of a preposition followed by the accusative case

   (b) two examples of a preposition followed by the ablative case.

9 From the last paragraph of the passage (lines 11–13), give and translate:

   (a) one example of a verb in the present

   (b) one example of a verb in the imperfect

   (c) one example of a verb in the perfect tense.

10 Translate the passage into English, writing your translation on alternate lines.

In the passage above, note the tense used after the adverb dum.

dum ... quaerunt (lines 5–6)

dum (= while) is generally followed by a present tense in Latin which should be translated by an imperfect tense in English.

E.g. dum ambulat = while he was walking.

The perfect tense of sum

Now that you know how principal parts work, you will have no difficulty forming the perfect tense of any verb, however irregular the verb may be. As you would expect, the principal parts of the verb sum are very odd, but forming the perfect tense is very simple, so long as you know the principal parts:

sum, esse, fuī = I am
fu-ī
fu-istī
fu-it
fu-imus
fu-istis
fu-ērunt

Exercise 8.17

Translate into Latin:

1 I have been good.

2 You (sing.) have been bad.

3 He has been tired.

4 She has been wretched.

5 We have been slaves.

6 You (pl.) have been masters.

7 The crowd has been savage.

8 The place has been sacred.

9 The messengers have been wretched.

10 The farmers have been tired.

Vocabulary 8

Latin	English
Nouns	
locus, -ī, m.	place
turba, -ae, f.	crowd
Numerals	
quārtus, -a, -um	fourth
quīntus, -a, -um	fifth
sextus, -a, -um	sixth
septimus, -a, -um	seventh
octāvus, -a, -um	eighth
nōnus, -a, -um	ninth
decimus, -a, -um	tenth
Verbs	
dēleō, -ēre, dēlēvī, dēlētum	I destroy
iubeō, -ēre, iussī, iussum	I order
maneō, -ēre, mānsī, mānsum	I remain
respondeō, -ēre, respondī, respōnsum	I answer
teneō, -ēre, tenuī, tentum	I hold
terreō, -ēre, terruī, territum	I frighten
cōnstituō, -ere, cōnstituī, cōnstitūtum	I decide
cōnsūmō, -ere, cōnsūmpsī, cōnsūmptum	I eat
lūdō, -ere, lūsī, lūsum	I play
ostendō, -ere, ostendī, ostentum	I show
pōnō, -ere, posuī, positum	I place

The story of Cloelia

After Horatius had valiantly defended the city against the Etruscan army (Chapter 6), and Mucius Scaevola had demonstrated his bravery by putting his hand in the flames (Chapter 7), Lars Porsenna concluded a truce with Rome. It was clear to him that the Romans were a force to be reckoned with.

At the time, he was keeping a number of Roman citizens captive, and one day, one of these, a young girl called Cloelia, decided to escape. She and a group of women slipped down to the river and swam across to safety on the other side.

> This topic is part of the Non-Linguistic Studies section of the ISEB syllabus.

However the Romans, as well as being fierce warriors, were honourable, and did not wish to break the truce. They therefore praised the brave girls for escaping, but then reluctantly sent them back to Lars Porsenna, explaining that to allow them to remain in Rome would be to break the truce that they had signed.

Lars Porsenna, once again, was overwhelmed by the Roman spirit, and sent Cloelia and her companions, and many more besides, back to Rome. Shortly after this, he withdrew his besieging army and the war that he had been waging on behalf of Tarquinius Superbus was at an end.

Exercise 8.18

1 (a) Tell the story of Cloelia in your own words.

   (b) What do we learn about the Roman character, and that of Lars Porsenna, from this story?

2 (a) Tell the story of Odysseus in the land of the Lotus-eaters.

   (b) How might Odysseus's story have been different if he had eaten the lotus plant, as his companions did?

9 Subordinate clauses; imperatives

Subordinate clauses

As we have already seen, sentences can be made up of more than one clause, joined by a conjunction.

E.g. puella cantat et servus rīdet = The girl is singing and the slave is laughing.

In this sentence, the two clauses make perfect sense on their own, but have been joined together into one sentence by the conjunction 'and'.

But very often, one clause in a sentence is subordinate to another. In such cases, the subordinate clause (in italics below) would make no sense on its own.

E.g.   The slave is laughing *because the girl is singing*.

        The slave laughs *when the girl sings*.

Two common types of subordinate clauses are temporal clauses, which tell us *when* something happened, and causal clauses, which tell us *why*.

1 Temporal clauses
   A temporal clause in Latin may be introduced by the adverb ubi = when and tells us *when* something happened.
   E.g. dominus, ubi īrātus erat, servum terrēbat.
      The master, when he was angry, terrified the slave.

2 Causal clauses
   A causal clause in Latin may be introduced by the adverb quod = because and tells us *why* something happened.
   E.g. dominus, quod īrātus erat, servum terrēbat.
      The master, because he was angry, terrified the slave.

The only slight difficulty with these clauses is the word order. In English we would probably say *either*:

   The master terrified the slave when he was angry.

or

   When the master was angry, he terrified the slave.

In Latin, however, the subordinate clause is often tucked inside the main clause. To help when translating, it can be helpful to put brackets around the subordinate clause.

E.g.   Rōmānī, [quod patriam vidēre cupiēbant,] ex oppidō discessērunt.

The Romans departed from the town because they wanted to see their fatherland.

Exercise 9.1

Translate into English (note that these clauses make no sense on their own):

1 ubi puer dormiēbat...

2 quod servī timēbant...

3 ubi rēgīna discessit...

4 quod legēbāmus...

5 ubi librum tenēbat...

6 quod dominum timuistī...

7 ubi in templō dormiēbātis...

8 quod turbam spectābam...

9 quod fortiter pugnābant...

10 ubi diū manēbat...

Exercise 9.2

Translate into Latin:

1 When he was walking...

2 Because he was tired...

3 When he was playing...

4 Because he was wretched...

5 When you (sing.) ran into the street...

6 Because you have destroyed the temples...

7 When you (sing.) were destroying the temple...

8 Because the horse was running...

9 When I saw the queen...

10 Because he did not answer...

Exercise 9.3

Translate into English:

1 fēminās saevās, quod hastās portābant, timēbāmus.

2 servus fessus, ubi dominum īrātum iterum vīdit, ē templō discessit.

3 quod rēgīnam nōn amābant, quīnque ancillae pecūniam cēpērunt.

4 incolae, quod Rōmānōs timēbant, per viās iterum festīnāvērunt.

5 Rōmānī, ubi Numa Pompilius regēbat, multa templa aedificāvērunt.

6 Rōmānī, quod perīcula nōn timēbant, incolās in bellum saepe dūcēbant.

7 ubi magister librum legēbat, quis puerōs parvōs ad agrōs dūcēbat?

8 ōlim rēgīnam, quod pecūniam cupiēbant, per viās iterum et iterum portābant.

9 ubi vīnum vīdērunt, septem nautae bibere cupiēbant.

10 poētae, quod aquam timēbat, undās magnās nōn ostendimus.

Adsum and absum

These two verbs are compounds of sum and are very easy to learn, as they go exactly like sum, with the addition of the prefix ad- or ab-.

adsum, adesse, adfuī = I am present	
Present	
adsum	I am present
ades	You are present
adest	He, she, it is present
adsumus	We are present
adestis	You are present
adsunt	They are present
Imperfect	
aderam	I was present
aderās	You were present
aderat	He, she, it was present
aderāmus	We were present
aderātis	You were present
aderant	They were present
Perfect	
adfuī	I have been present
adfuistī	You have been present
adfuit	He, she, it has been present
adfuimus	We have been present
adfuistis	You have been present
adfuērunt	They have been present

absum, abesse, āfuī = I am absent	
Present	
absum	I am absent
abes	You are absent
abest	He, she, it is absent
absumus	We are absent
abestis	You are absent
absunt	They are absent
Imperfect	
aberam	I was absent
aberās	You were absent
aberat	He, she, it was absent
aberāmus	We were absent
aberātis	You were absent
aberant	They were absent
Perfect	
āfuī	I have been absent
āfuistī	You have been absent
āfuit	He, she, it has been absent
āfuimus	We have been absent
āfuistis	You have been absent
āfuērunt	They have been absent

Exercise 9.4

Translate into English:

1 agricolae ab agrīs absunt.

2 nautae ā patriā diū aberant.

3 quis in templō adest?

4 cūr ā patriā abestis?

5 multī puerī et multae puellae in templō aderant.

6 ancillae, quod cibum cōnsūmere cupiēbant, prope dominum aderant.

7 poēta ā proeliō abesse cupīvit.

8 Rōmānī in proeliīs adesse semper cupiēbant.

9 turba agricolārum in agrō aderat.

10 quis in templō cum deā adesse cupit?

Exercise 9.5

Translate into Latin:

1 The sailor was absent from the war.

2 The inhabitants were present in the street.

3 I was absent from the fatherland.

4 You (pl.) were absent from the temple.

5 Often we are absent.

6 They have been present for a long time.

7 We have been absent for a long time.

8 The horse is absent from the field.

9 He always wants to be absent.

10 They do not want to be present.

Exercise 9.6

Study the passage below and answer the questions that follow.

Ulysses and the Cyclops Polyphemus

Ulixēs et sociī ad terram <u>ignōtam</u> nāvigāvērunt. ibi <u>spēluncam</u> magnam <u>invēnērunt</u>. ūnus nautārum 'quis in <u>spēluncā</u> habitat?' <u>inquit</u>. 'cūr nōn adest?' īn <u>spēluncam</u> Graecī, quod aquam et cibum cōnsūmere magnopere cupiēbant, intrāvērunt. subitō <u>sonum</u> magnum audīvērunt. <u>mōnstrum</u> saevum <u>appropinquābat</u> et īn <u>spēluncam</u> <u>ovēs</u> pellēbat. <u>mōnstrum</u>
5 saevum ūnum <u>modo</u> <u>oculum</u> habēbat: Cyclops, Polyphemus, fuit. Graecī perterritī īn <u>spēluncā</u> manēbant et <u>mōnstrum</u> spectābant. Polyphemus, ubi <u>spēluncam</u> <u>saxō</u> magnō <u>clausit</u>, virōs vīdit et clāmāvit. duŏ ē virīs cēpit et cōnsūmpsit. tum dormiēbat.
<u>postrīdiē</u> Polyphemus duŏ ē virīs iterum cēpit et cōnsūmpsit. tum <u>saxum</u> magnum mōvit et in agrōs <u>ovēs</u> <u>compūlit</u>. Ulixēs cum octo sociīs īn <u>spēluncā</u> manēbat. sociī perterritī erant. sed
10 Ulixēs, vir clārus et nōtus, nōn timēbat. <u>dum</u> <u>mōnstrum</u> abest, <u>pālum</u> magnum cēpit et <u>sicā</u> parvā <u>acuit</u>. tum, ubi Polyphemus iterum īn <u>spēluncam</u> vēnit, vīnum <u>mōnstrō</u> ostendit. 'vīnumne amās?' <u>inquit</u> Ulixēs. Polyphemus <u>pōculum</u> vīnī bibit et laetus erat. 'vīnum amō' <u>inquit</u>. '<u>alterum</u> <u>pōculum</u> vīnī cupiō!' Ulixēs <u>mōnstrō</u> <u>alterum</u> et tertium <u>pōculum</u> vīnī dedit. mox Polyphemus <u>ēbrius</u> erat.
15 'quis es?' inquit Polyphemus 'et cūr ades?' '<u>Nēmō</u> sum' respondit Ulixēs.
mox <u>mōnstrum</u> dormīre cupiēbat. <u>dum</u> dormit, Ulixēs <u>pālum</u> cēpit et in <u>oculum</u> <u>mōnstrī</u> saevī <u>ēgit</u>. statim Polyphemus clāmāvit. multī amīcī Polyphemī prope spēluncam habitābant et ad sonitum festīnāvērunt. clāmāvērunt amīcī: 'quis tē <u>vulnerat</u>? quis pugnat?' <u>inquiunt</u>. sed, ubi Polyphemus respondit '<u>Nēmō</u> mē superat! <u>Nēmō</u> mē <u>vulnerat</u>!' amīcī discessērunt.

ignōtus, -a, -um = unknown	modo = only	acuō, -ere, acuī = I sharpen
spēlunca, -ae, f. = cave	oculus, -ī, m. = eye	pōculum, -ī, n. = cup
inveniō, -īre, invēnī = I find	saxum, -ī, n. = rock	alter, altera, alterum = another
inquit = (he) said	claudō, -ere, clausī = I close	(of two), a second
sonus, -ī, m. = sound	postrīdiē = on the next day	ēbrius, -a, -um = drunk
mōnstrum, -ī, n. = monster	compellō, -ere, -pūlī = I drive	Nēmō = Nobody
appropinquō, -āre = I approach	dum = while	agō, agere, ēgī = I drive
ovēs (acc. pl.) = sheep	pālum, -ī, n. = stake	vulnerō, -āre = I wound
pellō, -ere = I drive	sica, -ae, f. = dagger	inquiunt = they said

1   Study lines 1–7 and answer the following questions.

   (a) Ulixēs … nāvigāvērunt (line 1): What are we told about Ulysses in these lines?

   (b) ibi … invēnērunt (line 1): What did he find there?

   (c) 'quis … adest?' (line 2): What two things did his companion want to know?

   (d) in spēluncam … intrāvērunt (lines 2–3): Why did the Greeks enter the cave?

   (e) subitō … appropinquābat (lines 3–4): How did the Greeks know that a monster was approaching?

   (f) mōnstrum saevum … fuit (lines 4–5): Give three things we are told about the monster.

   (g) Graecī … spectābant (lines 5–6): What did the Greeks do when the Cyclops approached?

   (h) Polyphemus … dormiēbat (lines 6–7): Give four things that Polyphemus did once he had entered the cave.

2   Translate lines 8–15 into English.

3   Study lines 16–19 and answer the following questions.

   (a) dormīre (line 16). What is the 1st person singular of the present tense of this verb?

      dormō   dormeō   dormiō   dormirō

   (b) cēpit (line 16). In which tense is this verb?

      Present   Imperfect   Perfect   Infinitive

   (c) saevī (line 16). In which case is this word?

      Nominative   Accusative   Genitive   Dative

   (d) clāmāvit (line 17). What would this word become if its subject were plural, keeping the tense the same?

      clāmant   clāmābant   clāmāverunt   clāmāvunt

   (e) habitābant (line 17). Which is the Latin subject of this verb?

      prope   amicī   Polyphemī   spēluncam

   (f) tē (line 18). What sort of word is this?

      Preposition   Adverb   Pronoun   Adjective

   (g) respondit (line 19). In which tense is this verb?

      Present   Imperfect   Perfect   Infinitive

   (h) respondit (line 19). What is the present infinitive of this verb?

      respondō   respondēre   respondāre   respondīre

   (i) discessērunt (line 19). What is the 1st person singular of the present tense of this verb?

      discessō   discessiō   discēdō   discēdiō

(j) Complete the following Latin sentence:

The inhabitant kills the friend.

incola _____ necat.

amīcus   amīcī   amīcum   amīcō

Imperatives

Imperatives are used to give orders or commands. They may be singular, if you are ordering one person, or plural, if you are ordering more than one.

	Singular	Plural
1st	amā	amāte
2nd	monē	monēte
3rd	regĕ	regĭte
4th	audī	audīte
Mixed	capĕ	capĭte

You may notice that these singular imperatives are simply the verb's present infinitive with the -re chopped off. The plural ones are formed from the 2nd person plural of the present tense, with the -tis changed to -te.

Exercise 9.7

Translate into English:

1 aedificā!

2 labōrāte!

3 intrā!

4 oppugnāte!

5 movē!

6 rīdēte!

7 discēde!

8 mittite!

9 audī!

10 venīte!

11 cape!

12 iacite!

13 dēlēte!

14 pōnite!

15 ostende!

16 regite!

17 stā!

18 laudāte!

19 bibite!

20 cōnsūme!

Give the singular and plural imperatives of the following verbs, with their meanings:

1	habitō	11	iubeō
2	currō	12	maneō
3	necō	13	respondeō
4	portō	14	teneō
5	habeō	15	lūdō
6	videō	16	ostendō
7	moneō	17	aedificō
8	regō	18	spectō
9	scrībō	19	festīnō
10	audiō	20	iaciō

Irregular imperatives

The imperatives of sum and its compounds are as follows:

sum	es	este
adsum	ades	adeste
absum	abes	abeste

You also need to learn the following three irregular imperatives:

dīcō	dīc	dīcite
dūcō	dūc	dūcite
faciō	fac	facite

And finally, note that the pronunciation of dō needs to be watched.

dō	dā	dăte

Note that plural imperatives are always formed in a regular way from the 2nd person plural of the present tense. It is only these singular imperatives that need to be learnt carefully.

Exercise 9.9

Translate into English:

Horatius holds the bridge

Etruscī Rōmānōs nōn amābant et oppidum oppugnāre cupiēbant. dominus Etruscōrum, Lars Porsenna, vir clārus erat. Lars Porsenna, multīs cum sociīs, ad oppidum festīnāvit et Rōmānōs spectāvit. Rōmānī prope <u>fluvium</u> aderant <u>nec tamen</u> cum Etruscīs pugnāre cupiēbant. <u>fluvius</u> inter oppidum et Rōmānōs <u>fluēbat</u>.

5   ūnus Rōmānōrum, Horātius, vir validus et nōtus erat. pugnāre semper amābat <u>nec</u> Etruscōs timēbat. sociōs, ubi Etruscī <u>appropinquāvērunt</u>, discēdere iussit. 'iam Rōmānī,' inquit 'trāns <u>fluvium</u> festīnāte et <u>pontem</u> dēlēte! egŏ Etruscōs nōn timeō.'

duŏ ē sociīs cum Horātiō adfuērunt, Titus Herminius et Spurius Lartius. trēs virī validī mānēbant et cum Etruscīs diū pugnābant. tandem Horātius iterum clāmāvit. 'trāns
10 <u>fluvium</u>, sociī validī, festīnāte!' <u>inquit</u>. duŏ virī validī trāns <u>fluvium</u> cucurrērunt. nunc Horātius sōlus cum Etruscīs stetit.

subitŏ, <u>sonum</u> magnum Horātius audīvit. Rōmānī gladiīs pontem dēlēvērunt et in <u>fluvium</u> <u>lignum</u> iēcērunt.

'<u>accipe</u>, domine <u>Tiberīne</u>,' inquit Horātius, 'socium tuum, etiam gladium et hastam, in aquās
15 tuās!'

deinde vir validus in aquam <u>dēsiluit</u>.

fluvius, -ī, m. = river	inquit = he said
nec tamen = but ... not	sonus, -ī, m. = noise
fluō, -ere = I flow	lignum, -ī, n. = timber
nec = and ... not	accipiō, -ere = I accept
appropinquō, -āre = I approach	Tiberīne (voc.) = Tiber (the river)
pontem (acc.) = bridge	dēsiliō, -īre, dēsiluī = I jump down

◯ Vocabulary 9

Latin	English	Latin	English
absum, abesse, āfuī	I am absent	itaque	therefore
adsum, adesse, adfuī	I am present	iterum	again
bene	well	mox	soon
deinde	then	ōlim	once upon a time
diū	for a long time	quod	because
etiam	also, even	saepe	often
fortiter	bravely	semper	always
hīc	here	sīc	so, thus
iam	now, already	statim	immediately
ibi	there	ubi	when

Coriolanus

This topic is part of the Non-Linguistic Studies section of the ISEB syllabus.

Rome spent much of its history at war with the neighbouring cities and tribes of Italy, and one such tribe was the Volsci. In 493 BC The Roman general Gnaeus Marcius captured the Volscian town of Corioli and acquired the name Coriolanus to commemorate his achievement. However, he became proud and tyrannical and, when he opposed the distribution of corn to the starving poor in Rome, he was driven from the city.

Ironically, he sought refuge with the Volsci, his former enemies, and in 491 BC he marched on Rome at the head of a Volscian army.

His mother was disgusted at her son's treachery and, taking his wife and children by the hand, marched into the Volscian camp where she confronted the traitor. She asked him whether he intended to murder his wife and children as well as his fellow citizens, and shamed by this, Coriolanus withdrew into exile.

Exercise 9.10

Find out as much as you can about Coriolanus. You might want to read about the play which Shakespeare wrote on the subject, or learn about the importance in Roman life of the family and loyalty to one's city.

1 (a) Tell the story of Coriolanus in your own words.

(b) What does this story tell us about the importance of the family in the Roman world?

2 (a) Tell the story of Odysseus and the Cyclops Polyphemus.

(b) Do you think this was the most dangerous of Odysseus's adventures on his return from the Trojan War?

■ Part of a painting of the Cyclops Polyphemus – from a bedroom at the Villa of Agrippa Postumus in Italy